RETIRE RICH, RETIRE EARLY

How To Retire At Any Age, For Real

Dr. Bruce M Firestone

B Eng (Civil). M Eng-Sci, PhD

How to Retire Rich at Any Age, For Real

A Learn By Doing School Book

Copyright © 2014 by Bruce M Firestone

All rights reserved, including the right to reproduce or transmit this book or portions thereof in any form whatsoever without written permission of the author and publisher.

For information, please contact:

Learn By Doing School Publications
Attention: Ms Nina Brooks, ninabooks@rogers.com
Tel 1.613.566.3436 x 200
@ProfBruce
www.brucemfirestone.com

First Edition

Firestone, Bruce Murray, 1951—

Booklet 2
How to Get Rich, For Real Series

Learn By Doing School Publications

Reviews for Real Estate Investing Made Easy

"I think Real Estate Investing Made Easy is a well written guide on how to enter the real estate market for any first time investor. As a serial entrepreneur who operates in a field that covers both real property and the IT space, I think the analysis provided by Prof Bruce offers readers a great framework. When I finished my engineering degree, I followed the bungalow split-level model personally and it has worked out fantastically. My location is near a college and I've have had 100% occupancy rates for the last five years. My IRR is in the 40-50% p.a. range(it includes capital appreciation). I really enjoyed Firestone's humorous, clear and personal approach in presenting the material. That's hard to find," Jason van Gaal, founder, planus.ca.

"Prof Bruce's Real Estate Investing Made Easy—How to Get Rich, For Real is an excellent resource. With particular attention to thoroughgoing calculations contained within, Professor Firestone has taken a complex investing vehicle (real estate) and explained it in simple terms which makes it a must-read for both experienced and novice investors. It will help many, many people build an investment foundation for a better future for themselves and their families on a daily basis," Daniel Casal, B Com (Hon) Finance.

"This book is really educational and informative for both beginner and advanced real estate investors. It was a great read. I love the fact that Firestone shares all the details related to these real estate deals, including calculations used to prove the numbers. Really educational and informative," Brent Mondoux, N-VisionIT Interactive.

Dedication

I dedicate this mini book to a client of mine—a single parent with three children (ages 3, 5 and 9) whose husband left her with nothing but the kids and a partially paid off house at age 36. Her name is Maya Yates*.

Maya has a decent job earning $84,000 annually but, like most people in the private sector, she does not have a defined benefit pension plan nor can she expect a lot of help from her former partner.

Maya with 1 of her 3 kids

She came to see me about a year after the split. Her question was, "What should I be doing to plan for my retirement?"

She knew that the longer the runway she had, the easier it would be because she'd read publications like David Chilton's 2011 book, *The Wealthy Barber Returns*. But she was having doubts about strategies espoused by many financial advisors—would they work for her?

Knowing I have a real estate background, she wondered if investing in property might work better for her and her children. We discussed her options and came to the conclusion that if she was ever going to be able to provide a viable retirement option for herself, it had to be principally through real estate.

To others who also don't feel that current retirement planning ideas are working for them, this booklet, *How to Retire Rich at Any Age, For Real*, is for you.

@ProfBruce
2014

"*I need to retire from retirement,*" Sandra Day O'Connor, retired US Supreme Court justice

(* Names, addresses and some numbers have been changed throughout this work to protect client privacy.)

Contents

Advance Reviews

Summary

Dedication

Introduction

What is a Life Worth?

Why You Can't Save Your Way to Retirement

Why Real Estate is a Unique Asset Class

Investment Success Story

Buying Low

Looking Back to See Ahead

Student Buys Her Own Home with Just $4,500

How to Buy Residential Rental Property, Smart—Don't be Lazy

Maya's Solution

Capitalization Rate

Internal Rate of Return

Value Proposition of a Residential Realtor

Value Proposition of a Commercial REALTOR

Why Use Mortgage Brokers?

Urban versus Suburban

Walkability Score Makes a Difference

Sub-Prime Blame

Conclusion

Addendum 1 Stocks or Real Estate?
Addendum 2 Due Diligence
About the Author

Summary

Developed nations are divided into three classes today—people, mostly government workers, with defined benefit pension plans which take all the risk out of their retirement, the top 1% who in 2012 had a 19.3% share of US national income (up from just 7.7% in 1973) and everyone else. This mini book is written for the latter—the 80% of the working population who have to fend (mostly) for themselves.

Financial advisors seem to be saying pretty much the same thing these days such as, "buy our mutual funds, use us to invest on your behalf in the stock market or stock market indices, buy our life insurance or term life products, cut your spending, save your money, let us invest your money for you in your 401(k) or IRA (RRSPs, TFSAs and IPPs in Canada), buy precious metals like gold through us…"

This book by Bruce M Firestone, PhD, lays out an alternative retirement strategy based on owning your own home plus three income properties. As the title says, it works at any age—whether you are 25, 35, 55 or even 75 although it works better at 35 or 55 than at 75. Today, the fastest growing demographic is 100 up so if you think that you may run out of retirement funds before you run out of runway, well, you could be right. What's interesting is the fact that people in the 25 to 30 age bracket are also getting with the program ending up with significant independent income by age 45 to 55.

How much money do you have to have to retire? Firestone looks at the case of Ms Maya Yates, a 36 year old single mother with a decent job who has set a goal of retiring at age 62 with an income similar to what she is currently earning—$84,000 annually.

She recently read a self help book that suggested she save 10% of her salary which she is having a tough time doing—she is responsible for three young children and gets no spousal support. She doubts this strategy will work for her anyway and she's probably right. Ms Yates knows that GE Capital Retail Bank's optimizer is currently offering 1.3% p.a. on their 3-year CDs (Certificates of Deposit) while Ally Bank offers 1.2%. This means that for Maya to create a retirement income of $84,000 annually for herself via CDs, she will need to save more than $6.7 million over the next 26 years. That works out to saving an impossible 3 times her current annual salary, not 10%.

Working with Ms Yates, Firestone's strategy involves selling her large suburban home, buying a less expensive but more urban one and using the balance of equity freed up that way to purchase three additional residential rental properties over a five year period.

Firestone takes the reader through the steps she takes to develop her mini real estate empire so she will be able to take care of herself and her family. He provides downloadable spreadsheets that show readers how to evaluate opportunities in real estate including how to properly calculate cap rates, internal rates of return and (cash-on-cash) returns on equity as well as wealth and inflationary effects. Dr Firestone talks about why you need to put a solid team together to help you get where you want to go and gives readers a few pointers on what to look for when investing in residential real estate as well as how to conduct due diligence during the conditional period preceding purchase of property.

He concludes by refuting the widespread argument that investment in housing was the root cause of the financial meltdown of 2008/09. Advice from senior bankers and politicians (most of them, perhaps all of them, homeowners themselves) suggesting that young people today not become homeowners runs counter to more than 60 years of national policy in most developed nations. These policies were designed to turn millennials and earlier generations into citizens with a stake in their societies and to protect them from financial calamites brought on by job loss, illness and divorce as well as economic and political upheavals.

Firestone puts it this way, "*Blaming high home ownership rates for the housing bubble and financial meltdown of 2008/09 is untrue and counter productive; it smacks of panic, craters resale and new home markets and destroys the dreams of the next generation hoping for a better tomorrow.*"

@profbruce

How to Retire Rich at Any Age, For Real

Introduction

I dedicated this booklet above to a single parent client (Maya Yates) who makes $84,000 per year; it's a decent job but, like around 80% of the modern workforce, it's one without a defined benefit pension plan which means that Maya won't be receiving an indexed pension for life that is guaranteed at a level independent of, say, the performance of the stock market or her employer. Those kinds of plans are available only to a privileged minority—mostly people who work in government or quasi-government positions. Even highly unionized industrial companies such as the auto sector don't provide defined benefit pensions any longer—the risk on the downside is all on the former employee's side.

Let's work through a checklist of some retirement options for Ms Yates—

1. defined benefit pension plan (not available to her)
2. other type of pension plan including 401(k), IRA, RRSP, TFSA, IPP, independent pension plan
3. investing in the stock market
4. investing in stock market indices
5. investing in mutual funds
6. developing a savings plan using t-bills, CDs, GICs or other savings vehicles
7. buying insurance or seg funds
8. investing in precious metals like gold
9. personal business for life
10. investing in real estate

Now if you are a government worker and have a defined benefit pension plan, you can still keep reading this book but the urgency of its message is really for everyone else, people who don't have what you have—something or someone who will look after them for the 20, 30 or even 40 years many North Americans can expect to live past 55.

Last year, I met another client who had done everything right—he'd bought a nice family home, paid off his mortgage and had more than $550,000 of savings in a self-directed IRA (individual retirement account). He is still working making around $150,000 per year and his health and energy level are excellent. Life is pretty good except he is 72 years of age and has come to realize that he cannot work at his current pace forever.

His mutual funds and stock market investments have been returning around 1% per annum over the last six years and some of his savings which are held in various bank accounts, t-bills and so forth are returning less than 1%. All of this to say, is that on his $550,000, he can expect about $5,000 per year in passive income to add to his existing pension of $895 per month and his spouse's which is just $545 per month. He has come to the realization that his generation and the two that are following him right now are completely out of luck. Freedom 55? More like freedom 85.

The Dow Jones, which is an indicator of overall condition of US stock markets, has averaged 0.52% before fees in the period 2000-2011. On an after fee basis, most investors have experienced negative returns. If you factor in inflation, returns are even more negative. With returns like this, you can never retire, *never*.

What's worse is that indices like the DJ, from time to time, remove companies that fail to meet their minimum requirements which means that the index has an inherent bias towards *overstating* returns. It's like you and I go to the racetrack to bet on horses but we only tell our friends about our winners. Not exactly an accurate portrayal of our ability to pick fast racehorses, right?

OK, so maybe stock market investing (whether picking individual stocks ourselves or having a professional advisor pick them for us either directly or by putting us into mutual funds or investing in stock indices) isn't going to provide sufficient returns for us to be able to retire rich. Maybe we could save enough instead whether inside an IRA, RRSP or TFSA or otherwise. How much money would that take?

What is a Life Worth?

When I was teaching in Sweden recently, I learned there was a baby boom going on. Strollers and kids were everywhere in Stockholm. Every girl I met between 18 and 40 either had a baby, was having one or planned to. It was nice.

Sweden's birth rate at 1.98 children per female is one of the highest in Europe (second only actually to France at 2.03). National polices that have been in place for decades not only make it easier for Swedish women to have a baby, but also find affordable childcare, good healthcare (for both mother and child) and keep her job.

Financial support is available not only for expectant mothers but also for her partner and both can stay home with a new baby for a year after birth.

Let's make a few assumptions. Say it costs Sweden 80,000 euros to support mother and partner in this adventure* and this investment produces one additional child.

(* The average wage in Sweden is about 28,800 SEK, Swedish Krona, per month. This is around $4,600 or 3,168 euros. If a mother and her partner are out of the workforce for a year, this amounts to a GDP "loss" of 76,032 euros. I have used 80,000 in this example.)

There were 115,641 babies born in Sweden in 2010 (a nation of 9.42 million) which means that their national government spent about $13 billion on child and mother (and partner) welfare if our assumption of 80,000 euros is right. That buys a lot of Swedish meatballs.

Is it worth it?

Since I have five great kids, I would answer "yes!" but then an economist has to provide something more substantive.

In November 2013, the SEB (Skandinaviska Enskilda Banken) fixed deposit 1-year rate was 1.27% p.a. So when a little Swedish girl grows up and makes an average annual salary, she will add 38,016 euros annually to Sweden's GDP which has a capital value* of €2,993,385.83 (this is 38,016 divided by 1.27%).

(* I am using the capitalization rate here which is probably right for this type of calculation since the residual value of a life is zero for most of us. For entertainers, artists and persons of historical importance, some of whom can make more money after they are dead, the equation would be different. More about the cap rate later.)

Worth €2,993,385.83?

Look at it this way—Sweden would need to deposit €2,993,385.83 in SEB fixed deposits for every child NOT born to equal the productivity of each new Swede who is born. So if Sweden's objective was to maintain its GDP even if there were no Swedes at all, it would need to come up with 346,158,130,393.70 euros EVERY YEAR to compensate for a society that produces no kids. Not only would a country without children be a horrible place to live, it would go broke.

So investing in kids should be a national priority and, in Sweden, it is.

But another way to look at it is that a JOB is *very* valuable. If you earn €3,168 a month, it is worth €2,993,385.83 to you. If you don't have a defined benefit pension plan that is fully indexed and don't feel you can rely on government or employer pension plans to support you as an elder, you will need to have 2,993,385.83 euros saved up to have the same lifestyle after you retire as before. That is hard to do. So staying at work as long as you can and planning on alternative forms of investing in addition to whatever type of pension plan you may have to provide for you after you do retire are important.

"Retirement kills more people than hard work ever did," Malcolm Forbes

The numbers in the US are similar while Canada's position is even starker. The average hourly wage in the US in November 2013 was $24.15 while in Canada (in October 2013) it was $26.14 for men and $22.58 for women.

A wage rate of $24.15 per hour implies an average annual salary of $48,300 in the US in 2013. GE Capital Retail Bank's optimizer offers a 1.3% p.a. coupon on 3-year CDs (Certificates of Deposit) as of December 31st, 2013 while Ally Bank offered 1.2% the same day. So to receive an equivalent salary through savings requires that the average person have $3,864,000 in her bank account. Now that is hard to do.

For a 2,000 hour work-year in Canada, average salaries are around $48,720. Taking the 17 *highest* institutional deposit accounts in Canada and averaging their 1-year GIC (Guaranteed Investment Certificate) rates give us a 0.823% return*. This means you would need to have $5,521,600 saved up to maintain your lifestyle after you retire in Canada. Even harder than what a Swede or American face.

(* http://canada.deposits.org/)

Why You Can't Save Your Way to Retirement

Investing in gold is almost as bad a retirement/investment strategy as the 2008 film *Fool's Gold* starring Kate Hudson and Matthew McConaughey is a movie. Rottentomatoes.com reports, "With little chemistry among the performers, humorless gags, and a predictable storyline, Fool's Gold fails on every level." They give the film a tomatometer score of just 11% with an average rating by viewers of 3.6 out of 10.

Rotten Tomato

In this section I deal with two issues—a) again why you can't save your way to wealth, you have to invest your way there and b) why "investing" doesn't mean speculating in precious metals like gold.

Many self help books advise you to save your way to a successful retirement. They make various recommendations like putting away 8, 10, 12 or 20% of your earnings every month and deferring spending or reducing spending. Keeping your on-going living costs down is very important. If your credit card balances are out of control and other debts are piling up, this is bad. Every dollar you *don't* spend is like $2 you *don't* have to make taking into account taxes you have to pay and other factors.

But here's the issue—almost no one can save their way to wealth. Here's why—

1. People who are good savers almost always find reasons to later spend those savings.
2. Life is uncertain and black swan events (emergencies) are less rare, more virulent and much more costly than bell-curve statistical theory predicts.
3. Returns on savings accounts and savings vehicles are at historic lows so they simply can't provide enough income to support you.

There is good debt and bad debt. Bad debt (like unpaid balances on credit cards) is unsecured. This means that if something happens to you like you lose your job or you get sick, you are still stuck with that debt, *personally*.

Good debt, like mortgage debt, is secured by an underlying asset which means that if you have to, you can sell that asset and the debt (in most cases) goes away.

So using debt to bolster your lifestyle is a bad idea but using debt to add assets to your portfolio can be a good idea provided that the asset also produces enough income to service and retire the debt over time.

That's why I am against other strategies like buying gold.

I went to a seminar two years ago at a university where I used to teach. I was invited there by the president of the university. She had a special guest coming to give a talk.

Most of these university talks are quite nice—sometimes informative, often entertaining. This one was embarrassingly worthless. The billionaire who gave the talk was hawking his gold fund to professors, staff and students. Perhaps the reason he was invited to speak had something to do with the twin facts that: a) he gave considerable amounts of money to the university and b) his name was on the building. But still, most of his audience was made up of young impressionable minds.

Investing in gold is *not* a retirement strategy. It hardly qualifies as an investment strategy either. It costs money to store it. It produces no income. It is not readily exchanged for goods or services—try going to your neighborhood food store and paying for your groceries with gold coins. You buy them for much more than the value of their gold content and you pay fees both when you buy and sell the things.

It is a hedge against the end of the world—if all else fails, having some gold might help your family in a world gone bankrupt but try negotiating your way out of a jam with, say, a zombie from the *Walking Dead*, or a motorcycle gang trying to rob you, might not work anyway.

The billionaire was talking up gold just as prices were peaking in the $1,800 to $1,900 per oz range in 2011. On the last trading day of 2013, gold was at $1,198.

A great hedge against inflation and awesome retirement plan, right? Just imagine what your portfolio would like you if you had borrowed money to buy gold at its peak.

"A common mistake that people make when trying to design something completely foolproof is to underestimate the ingenuity of complete fools," Douglas Adams

If you still think you would like to try a flyer on gold, take a gander at this spreadsheet first—

Gold Investing

Invest equity		$50,000			
Buy gold on margin		25%			
Total holdings of gold		$200,000	2011	$1,850	per oz
Total holdings of gold		$129,513.51	2013	$1,198	per oz
Debt		$150,000	2.55%	HELOC	15 yrs
Principal Repaid					
	1	($8,334.63)			
	2	($8,547.16)			
Total		($16,881.79)			
Debt Balance		($133,118.21)			
Invest equity		($50,000)			
Cash cost		($183,118)			
Value of gold holdings		$129,513.51			
Loss on investment		($53,604.70)			

Cash loss on investment	($70,486.49)

E&OE
Note:
Ignores transaction costs and fees as well as interest on HELOC
Download this spreadsheet here:
http://www.old.dramatispersonae.org/images/gold.xls

Now this is ugly. If you had followed the billionaire's advice and leveraged your home with a HELOC (home equity line of credit) to buy gold on margin, you would have taken $50,000 of your savings, added a $150,000 "mortgage" on your house to buy $200,000 worth of gold in 2011 that was worth $129,513 by the end of 2013 losing over $70k in just two years.

Do you know the fastest way to turn a billionaire into a millionaire? Buy a National Hockey League franchise. Still, this has to be the second fastest way.

Why Real Estate is a Unique Asset Class

Real estate has some attributes that are unique to this asset class. Here are ten of them:

1. You can rent real estate to third parties. (Try that with gold or stocks assuming you are not using exotic financial instruments.)
2. By renting to a third party you are benefiting from a 'wealth effect'; every year a renter is paying off part of your mortgage for you—when you sell that property, the decrease in principal owing goes into your pocket (assuming that the price you sell for is more than what you paid for the property plus transaction costs).
3. You receive unearned (and untaxed) rent on self-occupied property after your mortgage is retired.
4. When your city builds infrastructure around you, when your neighbors improve their properties, when the density and overall area of the city increases, demand for your property increases without you having done a thing—as a result your property value benefits from positive externalities.
5. In many countries, you are allowed to deduct a non-cash capital cost allowance against income—a significant tax advantage from holding real estate assets.
6. Real estate generally doesn't go out of fashion.
7. Land, unlike, say, ideas, is in fixed supply. (Many cities are further restricting supply by limiting urban expansion. Great if you are a sitting owner. Not so great if you are a first time homebuyer or newly minted entrepreneur.)
8. The amount of real estate consumed per capita has been steadily increasing almost everywhere for a long time as the total number of households increases due to higher divorce rates and other factors, contributing to longterm decline in average household size.
9. In-migration to urban areas from rural areas is continuing everywhere as cities benefit from network effects so overall demand for urban real estate is increasing secularly.
10. Lastly, real estate offers a unique opportunity to develop a sustainable business model even if you aren't a genius. Real estate develops a 'concession' or 'franchise' for its owners because once you own a particular location, axiomatically, no one else can own at that location.

Everyone knows that real estate is all about LOCATION, LOCATION, LOCATION but perhaps people don't realize why that is so crucial. For you to have a business that will nurture you and your family over a long period of time, you need to have some type of sustainable competitive advantage.

Imagine how difficult it is to run a company like Apple or how difficult it is to paint like Rembrandt. Not everyone can be a Steve Jobs or create artwork like Rembrandt Harmenszoon van Rijn. Real estate held in fee simple (the highest form of title an owner can have) gives you a franchise forever that tough competitors like Microsoft, Samsung, Apple or Google can't take away from you—IT'S A BUSINESS MODEL FOR DUMMIES like me.

A friend of mine owns a great commercial site—it's at a major intersection in a good part of town. He comes from a tech background but his chosen personal investment vehicle is real estate. He and his partner built a new, high concept strip mall (not intended as an oxymoron) on top of the old foundation of the previous building on site and, because of its high traffic location, great visibility and cool design features, they get rents that are about 1/3 higher than other nearby properties. I mean how difficult can it be to own a great location and have people come up to you, one after the other, to offer you top dollar for your space, year after year?

Investment Success Story

Real estate as an investment vehicle and as one of the key pillars of a successful retirement strategy is beginning to catch on with independent financial planners—ones who are not told by large financial services companies what financial products they are going to cram down your throat this season.

Here's a success story written by Scott Devries, BA, CIM, FMA, of Wealth Innovations who embraced a new private equity and real estate strategy for many of his clients.

In 2009, I began to research real estate as an investment option for client portfolios. Clients were starving for income and interest rates were at historical lows, directly impacting bond and savings yields, so earning reasonable income on the fixed income portion of their portfolios was challenging at best. While some investment structures did provide more income, they were directly linked to publicly traded markets and were subject to corrections in their valuations. For example, the REIT (Real Estate Investment Trust) market corrected approximately 30% in 2008.

Through these market downturns, what I observed was that home prices remained quite stable in our area. At the same time, a local broker asked me to look at a real estate investment opportunity for my clients that involved direct ownership of residential real estate with full property management. The targeted annualized cash yields were between 5% and 6% p.a. which seemed modest; however there was direct equity participation on the sale of the home that would likely bring double digit total returns.

Here was the issue the broker was presented with—his client was in difficulty in 2008/09. His business in the US was down and he had a residential building that he couldn't sell using the MLS system—it had to be a private sale. So what to do? We needed to organize a group of investors to help an entrepreneur buy below market and, then operate the property effectively and finally sell it when markets turned up. What did investors get? Excellent management and a terrific ROI over a 44-month period.

After analyzing the opportunity and completing due diligence, I ultimately recommended to a couple of high net worth clients (both dentists) that they invest in the project, which they subsequently did. The project had a four year investment horizon which seemed reasonable and I felt that it would help diversify their portfolios.

The property did not go without challenges in that the original tenant had some health issues and had to leave and the next tenant failed on their rental commitment and we had to evict them. This was done seamlessly through the property management team and required no action from investors.

Despite these challenges, the model worked perfectly. The home was sold in September 2013. Investors doubled their money over the term providing an annualized return of 24.6% on a hassle-free basis. Despite all the volatility in the markets during that time, we were able to secure both cashflow and capital appreciation for investors.

In the last several years, I've been working extensively on mortgage structures and alternative investments that I believe will help meet investors income requirements and preservation and growth of capital objectives. While I am not suggesting equity markets should be ignored, I believe it is the successful diversification of these asset classes that will lead to investor success.

We target returns of 8-12% with the security of having our clients registered on title. This solves both their income requirements and their goal of increasing their net worth.

While clearly we cannot expect 24.6% annualized returns on every investment, real estate affords us the opportunity to create both solid cashflows and capital appreciation with investments secured against real property. Solid, dependable returns is why in many countries nearly two thirds of their richest families have all or substantially all their wealth in real estate.

Buying Low

How do you buy low/sell high in real estate (and nearly everything else)? Here's how—

* Buy before the trough of the market
* Sell before the peak of the market
* Buy when everyone else is selling
* Sell when everyone else is buying
* Buy what no one else is buying
* Sell what no one else is selling

It's easy to say but hard to do. Why? Because everyone is highly influenced by what other people are doing and talking about so most people cycle up and down together. They buy when everyone else is buying and sell when everyone else is selling. They tend to buy what everyone else is buying and, hence, only have what everyone else has to sell when it comes time to sell. This tends to lead to buying high and selling low. Lenders are subject to the same influences which mean they only lend when everyone is buying which makes matters worse— cycles get peakier and trough'ier.

Counter-cyclical buyers or sellers resist these psychological pressures and have developed alternative sources of finance which gives them a degree of freedom to pursue their own strategy.

Warren Buffet is a good example of this philosophy albeit applied in (mostly) non real estate investing.

The 'buy before the trough' and 'sell before the peak' concepts are a bit harder to understand. If you decide to wait for the absolute bottom so you can get property at its absolute cheapest or the very top to squeeze the last dollar from a buyer, by the time you get there (to the bottom or the top of a cycle), market psychology has changed either for the better or for the worse so you can't actually buy at the bottom or sell at the top. You must act before, hopefully just before.

Looking Back to See Ahead

I have done a lot of spreadsheets for clients (using IRR, the Internal Rate of Return to measure real estate returns) for a Buyer about to purchase residential or commercial property—to give them some idea what rate of return they can expect from their investment. But recently I had the opportunity to do one for a couple of investor friends of mine who were thinking of divesting one of their residential properties by looking *back* to measure their return on investment.

The subject property is on a nice residential street; it has five bedrooms and two full baths; it is rented out to students from a nearby college on a room by room basis. Because of this, they are exempt from local rent control—they are free to raise rents as they see fit and evict roomers with a minimum of fuss if they are troublesome.

They are active landlords in the sense that they are over at the rental property at least once a month and they keep a close watch on their tenants. They paint each room when it becomes vacant and have a good relationship with the students.

We prepared a CMA (Comparative Market Analysis) for them and the value of the property, based on what comparable homes have sold for in the neighborhood in the last eight months, was estimated to be between $289,000 and $299,000. They were not particularly happy with the news that their property had not appreciated more.

In fact, they looked at it this way—the property had 'only' increased in value by $19,826 after deducting prospective agency fees for listing and sale plus closing costs (basically legal fees). With a purchase price of $262,000 in 2005, this seemed to our clients like a pretty puny increase in the four years that they had owned it. By their calculation, they had only seen a return of around 2.8% p.a.

(Subject calculations are shown below. For a more useful tool, download the spreadsheet in .xls format from our server, http://www.old.dramatispersonae.org/images/ResidentialSellersSpreadsheetCapRateIRR.xls.)

Now these folks are bright, talented people but the analysis they did on the spot was far from complete. First of all, they will make (assuming that it sells in the range we expect it to) $19,826 not on the original purchase price of $262,000 but on the cash equity they actually put up to buy the building, which was $65,000. So right away, the rate of return jumps significantly from 2.8% to 6.88% p.a. Not especially great but certainly better than you could get from your bank savings account or on a t-bill or CD.

Next, they had "forgotten" that they were cash positive throughout—their cash on cash return amounting to an average of about $645 per month. This yielded them a second return on their equity (ROE) of an additional 11.9% p.a.

Lastly, every month that they owned the house, their tenants were helping them pay down their mortgage. This is a wealth effect or, in an owner-occupied building, a form of forced savings. This amounted to another $18,911 paid off during their ownership period—a third form of return. Their ROE from this is around 6.6% p.a.

So if we now simply add up their three types or return (real estate inflation (all of which goes to the equity holder and none of which goes to the mortgage company), their cash on cash return plus the benefit they receive from the paydown of their mortgage), we get an estimated total ROE of 25.4% p.a.

Now this is just an estimate; to get a clearer picture, we need to use a somewhat more advanced technique—we need to measure IRR (the Internal Rate of Return) for their project.

When we do this, the IRR comes out a little bit lower: it is 22.6% p.a. (The reason it is lower than the ROE is because the IRR calculation properly takes into account the time value of money. For example, a cash on cash return of $7,744 is more valuable to our investors in year one than in year four.)

But still, a 22.6% p.a. is a lot higher than what you could get at the bank and a lot more than their initial view that they had only seen a return of "2.8%". (It is also a heck of a lot better than they did with their stocks and mutual funds which just a few years earlier had dropped 27% in a single year.)

Now there are a lot of assumptions that are implicit in these calculations like, say, we did not put in a fee for their monthly management of the building. Also, there is very little in here for marketing. (It turns out that Kijiji and other free websites were pretty much all they needed for this well located property anyway.)

The happy news is that the spreadsheet gave them confidence that, if they do decide to sell, they have done not so badly after all.

It is also interesting to note that the cap rate (capitalization rate = NOI/SP, where NOI is Net Operating Income and SP is Selling Price) is just 8% p.a. Cap rates are a rule of thumb that has a lot of traction in the real estate industry but it does not capture real estate inflation nor does it take into account the wealth effect from forced savings/paydown of the mortgage so it is a somewhat limited tool. Indeed, it is better for comparing one possible real estate investment with another than it is a measure of overall return from a real estate project. More on this later.

(* Note: Again, numbers and facts have been changed somewhat to protect the identity of the property and clients. Also note that this analysis is done before tax. Since tax calculations can be complex and highly subject to individual situations, each reader is advised to look at the tax implications of asset selling with their accounting advisor.)

129 Anywhere Crescent

Purchase Price $262,000 2005
Equity ($65,000)
Mortgage $197,000
Rental or Imputed Rent $2,200 per month $550 per month 4 bedrooms
$26,400 per year
Property Taxes ($2,489) per year 0.95%
Vacancy ($1,452) per year 5.50%
Marketing ($118.80) per year 0.45%
Insurance ($1,310) per year 0.50%
NOI $ 21,030.20 per year
Cap Rate 8.0% per year

IRR
Equity ($65,000)
Mortgage $197,000 4.50% 25 year amortization
($1,107.12) per month
($13,285.49) per year
Year
0 ($65,000) 2005
1 $ 7,744.71 2006 $ 645.39
2 $ 7,744.71 2007
3 $ 7,744.71 2008
4 $111,483.12 2009
IRR 22.6% per year cash on cash return + real estate inflation + forced savings (paydown of mortgage) Total Return
$ 30,978.85 $ 19,826.71 $18,911.69 $ 69,717.25
Principal Repaid ($4,420.49)
($4,619.41) Original Equity $65,000 $84,826.71
($4,827.28) Real Estate Inflation $ 19,826.71 (net of realty fees and closing costs)
($5,044.51) ROE(1) 6.88% $ 84,820.17
Total Principal Repaid ($18,911.69) Cash on Cash $ 7,744.71
ROE(2) 11.91%
Paydown of Mortgage $18,911.69 $83,911.69
ROE(3) 6.60% $ 83,934.82

Real Estate Inflation 3.25% per year 25.39%
Selling Price $297,756.69 after 4 years
Real Estate Fees ($14,887.83) 5%
Legal Fees & Closing Costs ($1,042.15) 0.35%
Net Selling Price $281,826.71
E&OE

Student Buys Her Own Home with Just $4,500

It can still be done. That is, young people can still buy a home with little money down, pay less than they did when they were renting, participate in real estate returns (inflation, forced savings and imputed rents) and get a stake in their society through home ownership.

Here is the story of one of my former students as written by her on her recently completed transaction. Names have been changed.

What went right?

• Using a mortgage broker was a great decision. Not only did we save our credit scores from being pinged countless times, it was also a painless way to get the job done. We didn't have to concern ourselves over what was needed because the broker always kept us up to date on what to have and when. This is especially nice since buying a house can involve many time-consuming steps. Eliminating this one was a godsend.

• Another thing that went right was our choice of lawyer. We chose my family lawyer (I'll call him Ben), and although we did end up paying more than if I had shopped around, I found that trust was much more important than saving a few dollars. My parents have been using the same lawyer since I was born and they have complete faith in his abilities, which was more than enough for me.

For example, while doing the home inspection, we found that the building had no central air conditioning, whereas the feature sheet said that it did. This had been a big selling point for us and we were disappointed. Ben found this out the day of the inspection through a third party and called us within an hour with legal advice as to how to proceed. He had done some research on how much A/C units cost, determined how old it would have been (had it existed) and gave us an opinion on how the sellers could address this issue. (They ended up giving us a $1,500 discount on the price.) Our lawyer was not obliged to do this extra work for us but you get what you pay for! Those few extra dollars really paid off.

What went wrong?

• It was beyond our control but the whole process was thrown off because our sellers were being represented by a, dare I say it, incompetent realtor. I will call him Joe. Joe was never available for communications, he had knowingly misled us on the feature sheet and was rude and hot-headed. This not only inconvenienced us but the sellers were also hurt when they were required to lower their price because of the A/C issue. Joe couldn't even give our agent the right lock box code. We stood outside the place for ten minutes trying variations to no avail. Naturally, Joe didn't answer his phone either. Lucky for us (and the sellers), they were across the street watching us trying to get in. They came across the road and let us in with their house key. If it weren't for this bit of luck, they wouldn't have sold their home and we wouldn't have bought it.

From my experience and from what I have heard, it is not that difficult to find a good agent. The sellers found Joe at an open house and signed on with him immediately. I admit that is how I found my agent too but I did some due diligence. I researched her a little more before signing on. It is crucial that you have a good agent or everything can spin out of control, so do your homework.

All in all, I would recommend buying over renting to any of my friends, almost no matter what their financial situation is. My boyfriend once said that all you need to buy a home is, "lots of money and patience" but I would say that the only thing you actually need is patience. It is a lengthy process but you don't need to be rich to go through with it.

How we did it (and hopefully my mortgage company doesn't read this) is through "creative accounting"… and don't worry, it's not Enron's version of creative.

I had been able to finish university without any debt, meaning I had the majority of my $10,000 student line of credit still available to me. The interest rate on it is quite low so I wanted to make use of it. For the house we wanted, our down payment came to $9,000 between the two of us (my boyfriend and me), making it only $4,500 each. This is more than reasonable considering what we get from it. But unfortunately you are not allowed to use borrowed money to make your downpayment. Therefore, we used our trusty parents to make the downpayment with the promise that, in time, the money from my line of credit will [somehow] make it into their bank accounts. This way the mortgage company gets their money, the bank gets their money, my parents get their money and everyone is happy. In my eyes, $4,500 is inexpensive for such a large investment and now we are paying less every month in mortgage payments than we ever did on rent.

How to Buy Residential Rental Property, Smart—Don't be Lazy

Here are a few tips for readers who are thinking about acquiring some residential rental property to consider before they do.

"Nothing will work unless you do," Maya Angelou.

a) **Get a property manager** who carefully vets tenants. You are far better off to leave a place vacant than to rent to a bad tenant. If you do have a poor tenant, an experienced property manger will know how to navigate the process to evict them.

b) **Don't ever buy a property that doesn't cashflow**. The idea that you can make up for monthly cashflow deficiencies by capital appreciation is flawed. It will crater your IRR, Internal Rate of Return.

c) **Buy low/sell high.** You make money in real estate when you buy not when you sell. So if you get in a competitive situation and get carried away and pay too much for that cool triplex or duplex, you're sunk.

d) **Try to use all the leverage you can**—financial institutions in many nations will still lend to people with good credit (i.e., decent Beacon Scores) with just 5%, 10% or 15% down. So rather than buy one residential unit with 25% down, you could buy five of them with 5% down on each or two of them with 12.5% down. Using more leverage now will eventually allow you faster de-leveraging later assuming all your properties cashflow.

e) **If you own five units and one becomes vacant**, your vacancy rate has jumped from 0 to 20% which is probably manageable but if you only own one unit and it becomes vacant, your vacancy rate has leapt from 0 to 100% which is bad.

f) **By using lots of leverage, you actually will have way more cashflow and more forced savings and more wealth effects** provided you live in a stable economic environment (like, say, Boston, Portland or San Francisco not Arizona, Nevada, Florida or California) and provided you followed my earlier rule—buy low.

g) **You or your property manager should visit** each of your rentals, once per month. Tell your tenants in advance (some jurisdictions require you do this in writing) that you will visit once per month to collect rent *personally*, to inspect the unit every time you visit and to fix any problems immediately. Don't be lazy, do it. If prospective tenants don't want this, no problem. They can rent somewhere else. Those friends of mine with that 5-bedroom home near a college which was rented out to students, they visited every month bringing dinner with them (kids are always hungry). They developed solid relationships with their tenants, monitored the condition of the place, never lost a single month's room rent and even helped them with homework and personal problems when warranted.

h) **When I owned a rental property in a tough neighborhood, I co-opted the locals** including teens by hosting a FREE BBQ and blocko (short for block party) every summer. I gave all the kids (some of whom were gang members no doubt) free burgers and flying discs and told them if they needed anything to let me know. In the years I owned the place, I had zero graffiti and vandalism—the locals looked out for it for sure. The few hundred bucks it cost was much less expensive than higher insurance premiums and repair bills. (Note: you can often get a permit to close a street for a blocko from your local municipality. They're usually free. You can invite everyone in the area by the simple expedient of a flyer drop (in some neighborhoods like the one we were in, websites/mobile apps/email/facebook/twitter/linkedin/online invitations just aren't going to work). Free food and beverage with some music and games (we liked Ultimate played on the street and Paddle Tennis) will bring people out for sure. But don't serve any alcohol—this leads to fistfights and opens you up to huge liability.)

i) **You can add in-home residential apartments to your principal residence and to your rentals.** If it's your principal residence, it has the useful advantage that you don't have to travel very far to keep an eye on the place plus part of your mortgage interest (if you still have one) becomes a business expense since you are earning income from your place. In the US, mortgage interest is already tax deductible. In Canada, your principal residence will still be capital gains tax exempt as long as the apartment is contained within the original footprint of the building, i.e., in the basement or attic say. There is government support for the cost of adding in-home rental apartments in the form of CMHC grants/loans (up to $25,000) but most of the in-home apartments that I've seen added over the years make financial sense even without soft loans or grants. Also, many cities and towns have legalized them, in part, to bring them out of the grey market and, in part, to provide more affordable housing. Legalizing them has made compliance with local building codes more likely and improved the safety of these places. I lived in a place like that when I was at UCSC many years ago and one of the granny flat plans we developed is a riff on that little place, located I still remember, at 1011 and ½ Seabright Avenue in Santa Cruz, California. If you would like to see some of those plans, let me know either via @ProfBruce or @Quantum_Entity on Twitter.

j) **If you build or buy a duplex/triplex/multiplex, make sure you sound, smell and fire separate** your units and they comply with all building, health, fire and safety codes. If you are purchasing an existing building, make sure you have a building inspector who knows these codes and can provide you with advice and costs estimates to make your units legal. If you discover any surprises, it's best to find these out during your conditional (due diligence) period when you can either abandon the deal or ask for a price abatement from the seller. Fire separation is improved by adding an extra layer of drywall. If you add it so that sheet boundaries do *not* line up, you will improve not only fire protection, you will limit sound transmission and smells between units. There are lots of simple, inexpensive things that you can do that not only improve safety for your tenants; they make their lives more enjoyable. If you are careful not to vent one unit into another, for example, you automatically reduce sound, smell and fire issues...

k) **Residential real estate returns come in three pieces:** positive monthly cashflow (aka cash on cash return) when rental and other income (like parking or laundry revenues) exceed expenses, forced savings/wealth effects (every month you pay your mortgage, actually, when your tenant pays your mortgage for you, you end up paying a bit of the principal off) and inflation (which comes from capital appreciation—i.e., when you sell for more than you bought).

l) **Put together a really good real estate team to advise you**—experienced coach, knowledgeable residential (and later commercial) real estate broker or salesperson, thorough building inspector who can not only tell you what's wrong with a building but how to fix it and how much that might cost, deal making lawyer, fair appraiser (who is working for you not the lender), honest, innovative and competent contractors/renovators, creative interior designer and home stager, landscaper, decent property manager, plugged-in mortgage broker... More about your real estate team later.

Maya's Solution

The Challenge

According to the latest US census, poverty is on the rise for households headed by single mothers. In fact, 4.1 million single mother families representing 41.5% of all such female-headed households were poor in 2012, continuing a four year trend of secular increases in poverty rates for this group. Upward social mobility has declined and more people are falling into the lowest income group after five years of decreases in homeownership.

The US has one of the lowest social mobility scores amongst developed nations and one of the highest rates of economic inequality. This means that if you are born into a poor family, you are likely to remain poor and the top 1% of the population's share of national income is 19.3% (in 2012) up from just 7.7% in 1973. Miles Corak's Gatsby Curve shows that social mobility in the US is lower than France, Spain and Japan and much lower than rates in Canada and Nordic nations Finland, Norway and Denmark. Income inequality in the US is greater than in almost all other developed nations according to Corak.

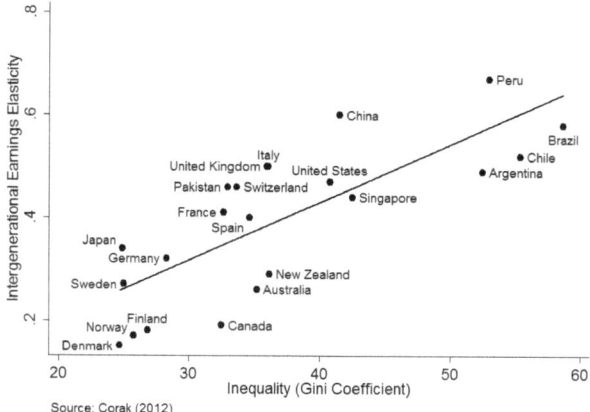

Source: Corak (2012)

This is a stark warning not only to Ms Yates and her three children but to all families whether female-headed or not. Despite the widespread blame heaped on sub-prime loans provided to persons with less than stellar credit ratings to purchase homes, the recession of 2008/09 and the accompanying financial meltdown were *not* caused by home loans per se. The meltdown was caused when fraudulent financial products were pushed on unsuspecting investors by financial services firms backed up by credit rating agencies who labeled portfolios of home mortgages as triple-A when in fact they were anything but.

We will discuss this in more detail in the conclusion but it is my view that homeownership is not only a sensible national policy goal, it is imperative for bringing people out of poverty and not just in the developed world. One of the greatest development economists of our time, Hernando de Soto, says that by unlocking capital within informal settlements (ones that governments and NGOs used to call slums) by surveying these areas and conveying ownership to residents living there with clear title, nations can bootstrap themselves and their emerging entrepreneur class out of intense cycles of poverty. Afterall, the number one source of startup capital, worldwide, is home equity and it's the entrepreneurs class in every nation that leads the population out of poverty.

So in speaking with Maya, I asked her what her goals were. She answered that she would like to retire at 62 (she was 36 when we first spoke) with an income equivalent to what she currently makes—around $84,000 per year. I told her that most retirees can make do with about 60% of their working income after they retire because their costs are usually much lower—less debt, fewer responsibilities.

Her youngest child would be 29 by then and presumably self-supporting. She was adamant however. Her goal was income of $84,000 per year.

This would require, I told her, that she save $6,720,000 in the next 26 years assuming interest rates on CDs (currently around 1.25%) stay the same. Total savings required is calculated simply this way: $84,000/1.25%. Actually, she would only need to save $6,702,000 because she already had $18,000 in cash and marketable securities. This amounts to saving $257,769 *per year* (ignoring the measly 1.25% interest coupon for the moment) every year for the next 26 which is 3.07 times her total annual income. So financial advisors telling her to save a percent of her income, say 10%, to provide for her old age obviously can't do basic arithmetic.

Maya's situation is, in fact, a bit better than this. Her 401(k) plan will generate income for her and she will be eligible for social security at age 62 although she may elect to wait until age 67 to begin collecting a somewhat higher amount. Currently, social security payments in the US average $1,269 per month (2013) and she will be able to add an unknown amount to that via her 401(k). Let's assume that is $525 per month. So if her goal is $84,000 per year in retirement income, she will get $21,528 of that from social security and her 401(k) which leaves a discrepancy of $62,472 annually. So in fact, the amount she needs to save is (($62,472/1.25%) - $18,000) or $4,979,760 which works out to a savings requirement of $191,529 per year, still 2.3 times what she currently makes, an obvious impossibility.

So I said, "Let's work through an alternative scenario. One where you own your own principal residence and three other rental properties. Let's see what that does to the math and whether you can accomplish your goal that way instead." It might also be easier to do because I added, "In my opinion, you can't save your way to retirement, you have to invest your way there."

"OK," she said. "I'm listening."

Personal Balance Sheet

Next I asked her if she had a personal balance sheet. "Huh?" she answered.
So we put one together for her—

Personal Balance Sheet (Ms Maya Yates)

Effective Date:	Q4 2011
Assets	
Cash & Marketable Securities	$18,000
401(k) Plan	$101,096
Fine Art	$48,000
Jewelery	$14,000

Furniture	$39,000
Real Property (principal residence)	$685,000
Cemetery Plot (family)	$1,900
Vehicle	$6,000
Badge Amber (sales of Baltic amber bracelets on etsy.com)	$108,000
Total Assets	$1,020,996
Liabilities	
Mortgage (principal residence)	$305,000
Other Liabilities (credit card debt)	$18,000
Total Liabilities	$323,000
Net Assets	$697,996
Notes—	
Face Value of Life Insurance	
Maya Yates	$650,000

The longest lived institutions on this planet—House of Windsor, Emperor of Japan, Holy Roman Catholic Church, Hudson's Bay Company—all do it; they control their affairs using double entry bookkeeping: balance sheets, income statements and sources and uses of cash so why shouldn't you do it? (They also have most of their wealth in real estate.)

The personal balance sheet should be updated at least once per year. It is amazing what you can discover from it. For example, Maya was surprised to see $108,000 added to her personal net worth by yours truly for Badge Amber, her home-based business that she started with her oldest child (her 9-year old daughter, she has two girls and one boy) as a lark. She sells handmade amber bracelets, necklaces and anklets for adults and kids on etsy.com that promise to provide customers with "positive energy".

They made $900 per month net in the previous year which Maya has been using to pay for dance lessons for her two girls. It doesn't quite cover all those costs but it's close.

Well, $900 per month is $10,800 per year which using a capitalization rate of 10% implies that Badge Amber is worth $108,000. This is a *notional* value. If she was to sell the business, she might only get one times revenue (for her designs, customer list, website, goodwill) so you could argue the figure should only be $10,800. But you could also look at it this way—it's worth $10,800/1.25% or $864,000 since that is the amount of savings she could displace if she is still running this micro business at age 62! So $108,000 seems fair and, in any event, it's a placeholder. Maybe when she is 62 and not caring for her kids or working full time, she could run Badge full throttle and make some real money. But for the purposes of this analysis, we are not counting on that.

Badge Amber is what I call a personal business for life (PB4L). It is my view that everyone should have one of these.

A personal business for life is a business owned by a single individual with no partners or at most one partner (most likely a family member) with little or no debt which uses small amounts of startup capital and provides real value to its stakeholders as well as having a close connection with its clients and customers as well as suppliers. A PB4L is never put at risk by taking on too much debt or by being over reliant on a single customer or supplier.

A PB4L, as my dad used to say, is an iron reserve—something that you can fall back on when all else fails. If you look at the definition above, the words "provides real value" and "being over reliant on a single... supplier" mean that I am excluding pyramid and multi-level marketing schemes. Things like, "I'll tell you how to earn a million dollars if you give me a dollar" and a million people do it, are not PB4Ls.

They have to be real businesses. One way to find inspiration I think would be to go get a copy (from your library) of the Encyclopedia Britannica and look for crafts from the 1930s. PB4Ls could be things like making specialty paper, selling nostalgia products like field notes (http://fieldnotesbrand.com/), writing a comic strip like former student Ryan North does (http://qwantz.com/index.php) then selling merchandise based on it, Badge Amber, writing mini books, getting a REALTOR license, urban farming (fruits, veggies, eggs), grass cutting, landscaping, personal support worker, hairdressing, bookkeeping, computer repair, car customization, window cleaning, painting, home repair, deck, fence and gazebo construction, games, toys, crafts, recipes, sign maker, consultant, life coach, mentor, vintage furniture... There are millions of ideas.

For more on PB4Ls, please see, http://www.eqjournal.org/?p=2020.

Principal Residence

Maya and I concluded that it might be the right move to sell her home. It was a 5-bedroom suburban monstrosity which needed lots of maintenance and repairs. Her property taxes were very high as well. Moreover, her kids couldn't walk anywhere; everything required Maya to drive them there. Public transit in her neighborhood is a joke. Also, by age 14 or 15, her kids might want jobs of their own and there weren't any employment opportunities nearby, not even a c-store where her children could work in entry-level retail.

If she sold her principal residence, she would be able to unlock equity in her home which she could then parlay into another (smaller, less expensive) principal residence and her first rental property. Of course, she could have remortgaged her home or put a HELOC (Home Equity Line of Credit) in place to get access to that money but she would still have been stuck with a suburban lemon.

She put it up for sale and six weeks later this was the result—

	Maya's 5-Bedrooom Suburban Home	
Asking price	$685,000	
Selling price	$672,500	
Commission	($33,625)	5%
Attorney fees	($875)	
Net	$638,000	
Mortgage	($305,000)	
Net net	$333,000	cash

She and her kids moved in with her parents during a three month transition period during which she bought and renovated a 3-bedroom split-level home located in the inner city in a rapidly gentrifying neighborhood. Her plan was to have her girls share a room while her son got his own bedroom as did Maya.

She also decided to add 2 more bedrooms and a bathroom to the lower level which conveniently had a walkout condition and separate entrance.

This is what her situation looked like afterwards—

Maya's 3-Bedroom Split-level Home

Asking price	$385,000		
Purchase price	$321,500		
Attorney fees	$875		
Pennsylvania state deed transfer tax	$3,215	1%	to buyer
Total cost	$325,590		
Upstairs renos	$35,000		
Lower level renos (add 2-bedrooms)	$48,000		
Total cost	$408,590		
Equity	($122,577)	30%	
Mortgage	$286,013		
Maya's cash on hand after purchase	$210,423		
Pay credit card balances	$18,000		
Maya's cash on hand after purchase	$192,423		

Now here's where it gets interesting. Her plan was to rent out each lower level bedroom, fully furnished, to mature students studying at a nearby university which had opened a center for corporate and executive education. She provided Internet and Netflix for two students each with their own bedroom. They shared the lower level's one bathroom, kitchen (with bar fridge, hotplate, toaster oven and small dining table seating four) and a living/TV room with comfortable, stylish but still second hand furniture.

This is what Maya's monthly cashflow looked like after her move:

Maya's Monthly Cashflow

Mortgage	$286,013		
Interest	2.99%		
Amortization	20	years	
Monthly payments	($1,554.10)		
			no
Property taxes (est)	($594.50)	$7,134	exemptions
Maintenance	($128.60)	0.04%	
Misc	($96.45)	0.03%	
Total monthly cost	($2,373.65)		
Lower level bedroom 1	$850	per month	
Lower level bedroom 2	$850	per month	
Total	$1,700	per month	
Vacancy allowance	($204.00)	12%	
Total	$1,496	per month	
Total monthly cost	($877.65)	per month	

So now Maya is living in her own home, providing a safe environment for her children and spending less than $900 per month to do it. How does this compare to her previous situation?

There is no comparison. If she had stayed in her suburban home, her monthly costs would have looked like this:

Maya's Suburban Monthly Cashflow

Mortgage	$305,000		
Interest	2.99%		
Amortization	20 years		
Monthly payments	($1,657.27)		
			no
Property taxes (est)	($1,218.67)	$14,624	exemptions
Maintenance	($538.00)	0.08%	
Misc	($403.50)	0.06%	
Total monthly cost	($3,817.43)		

Now any financial advisor who tells you that you should reduce your spending is telling you something that is right for almost everyone. Maya went from spending nearly $4,000 per month living in a suburban house she once shared with her partner to spending just $877 for what is a better lifestyle anyway. The wear and tear on her car not to mention herself is much lower as is her spending on gasoline.

But it gets better. Housing inflation in her new neighborhood is averaging 3.45% per year. Suburban homes are doing 1% at best. This means that by the time Maya is 62, her suburban home would have gone from a value of $672,500 to around $871,000. But compare this to what happens to her more urban-style home:

Comparing Urban and Suburban Home Values

Suburban House		$672,500		
Inflation		1%	p.a.	
Time Period	$	871,059.87	26	years
Urban Home		$408,590		
Inflation		3.45%	p.a.	
Time Period	$	986,916.94	26	years

Her split-level inner city home has more than doubled in value while providing her with some nice rental income plus she is much closer to services like stores, public transit and medical care which she may need later in life. And there is the fact that the nearly $1 million it will be worth forms a large part of her required "savings". Note that Maya didn't in fact "save" this, at least not in the conventional sense. As long as she pays her mortgage every month (actually she opted for two payments per month), Maya will arrive at her destination—a fully paid for home. It is a certainty. She traded a large relic of a house in exurbia for a split-level fixer-upper closer to the city center. She used some of the cash that she freed up to pay off "bad" debt (unsecured credit card debt). The rest she will use to buy rental property along with other investments including putting some into her 401(k) and into a reserve for emergencies.

So Maya isn't on her way to a rich retirement because she is saving her way there. No, she is investing her way there using OPM (other people's money). OPM in this case comes in three forms—firstly, she is using funds provided by her mortgage lender to leverage her equity.

Secondly, she is using her tenants' rental payments to cover some of her mortgage and monthly costs associated with her home. Lastly, remember that the 3.45% p.a. inflation in real estate is all hers (her lender gets none of the upside on her investment) which means her 30% equity is seeing an 11.5% p.a. return in her first year. She did nothing to earn this return other than continue breathing. Real estate rental curves in many inner cities have significantly higher upward slope than suburban curves (provided, of course, that there is an absence of crime—both petty misdemeanors and major felonies).

By retire rich, I don't mean the lifestyles of the rich and famous. I am using the word "rich" in the Jesuit fashion—I am talking about *tantum quantum*, St Ignatius's principle which stated, "We are to use them in so far as they lead us to our last end, and be rid of them in so far as they hinder us in the pursuit of the end for which we were created." Ignatius was talking about creatures but it is also true about possessions. In more modern terms, it would be said this way, "Take what you need and no more."

Oh, by the way, the reason that Maya got such a good deal on her split-level (asking price of $385,000, purchase price of $321,500) is the fact that she bought it from a lady who is a hoarder. The place (to be kind) didn't show well and had been on the market for more than a year but it had good bones and Maya wasn't afraid to do the work it took to clean up and renovate the place.

Her First Rental Property

As Freddie Bauer (John Candy's character in the film *Splash*) once said, "Hey, when I find something that works, I stick with it!" So Maya looked for another split-level in her neighborhood, one that she could buy, fix up and use as part of her long planned for rental portfolio.

Unfortunately, another stigmatized property in her local market was not available to her and prices there had gone up considerably since her first move. Nevertheless, the advantages (in terms of property management and maintenance) from being nearby outweighed a focus solely on cost. Still, she had to buy smart.

She ended up with a 5-bedroom split-level, again with 3 upper bedrooms and 2 lower. This one did not have a walkout condition but it did have a side door that landed a person at grade which meant that the lower level is only half a flight down. It also led to the upper level being a half flight up in high-ranch bungalow fashion. It also had a street-facing front door. This led to an interesting possibility—separating the upper and lower levels into separate apartments.

Maya added a kitchenette to the lower level and an inside door which could be locked on both sides making the side door exclusively for use by people tenanting the lower level.

The new home had a carport (but no garage) for one car with room enough to park two more (small) vehicles in series. Ms Yates removed the grass from the front yard and put in paving stones to reduce lawn maintenance (to zero) and also to provide another parking space at 90 degrees to the main driveway. It reduced the need for her prospective tenants to car jockey.

She repainted the place and added a few of her own design elements to make the two apartments homier including a gas fireplace in the lower unit. She did not furnish these units.

This is what her returns look like now—

Maya's Monthly Cashflow from 1st Rental

Mortgage payment	($1,365.98)		
Property taxes (est)	($733.75)		
Maintenance	($226.08)	0.06%	
Misc	($150.72)	0.04%	
Total monthly cost	($2,476.53)		
Rent (upper level)	$1,925		
Rent (lower level)	$985		
Total rent	$2,910		
Vacancy allowance	($146)	5%	
Total rent	$2,765		
Cash on cash return	$433.47	per month	
Cash on cash return	$5,201.64	per year	
Equity	($125,997.90)		
ROE, return on equity	4.1%	per year	cash on cash return
Real estate inflation	3.5%	per year	excluding mortgage payment
NOI, net operating income	$1,799.45	per month	
NOI, net operating income	$21,593.40	per year	
Total cost of purchase and renos	$419,993		
Cap rate	5.1%	per year	

IRR, internal rate of return

0	($125,997.90)		
1	$5,201.64		
2	$5,201.64		
3	$5,201.64		
4	$5,201.64		
5	$226,971.54	$247,778.10	

IRR		**15.3%**	**p.a.**	
Selling price of rental property	$	498,819.93	after	5 years
Attorney fees		($925)		
Realtor commission		($24,941.00)	5%	
Net	$	472,953.94		

Principal paydown

1	($8,063.66)			
2	($8,305.57)			
3	($8,554.74)			
4	($8,811.38)			
5	($9,075.72)			
Total principal repaid	($42,811.06)			
Equity	($125,997.90)	($8,562.21)	average per yr	
Wealth effect (average per annum)	6.8%	p.a.		

Balance on mortgage	$251,184.04

Now if you look closely at this spreadsheet, you can be forgiven for asking why her measured returns range from a low of 4.1% to a high of 15.3% per year. This is a big range. Maybe my spreadsheet skills need improving, you are thinking?

But the fact is that the way financial returns are calculated is subject to how you decide to measure those returns. If you are only concerned with how much cash you clear every month, you may decide to use a measuring stick based solely on ROE, return on equity. Since Maya is paying more for this home that she would have liked, her monthly cashflow is quite small—just $433 per month. This is money that, as my wife likes to say, you can touch, feel and spend. Based on the total amount of cash she invested in this property ($125,998 of equity), her cash on cash return (ROE) is just 4.1% p.a.

Her cap (capitalization) rate is a bit higher: 5.1% p.a. As you already know, cap rates are NOI, net operating income (before debt service) divided by selling price or purchase price. In this case, it is $21,593/$419,993. The purchase price should, in my view, include the cost of renos, attorney fees and state deed transfer tax to accurately reflect her real returns. These are very real costs and push down her cap rate.

Real estate inflation is 3.5% p.a. but remember all of this increase in value goes to the owner not the lender so in year 1, Maya sees an additional return of 3.5%/30% or 11.7% p.a. This is a non cash return in the sense that you only realize it when you either sell or refi (refinance) your building.

Lastly, Ms Yates is experiencing a wealth effect. Her tenants are paying down her mortgage for her. Over 5 years, total principal repaid is $42,811 or an average of $8,562 per year leaving a balance owing on her mortgage of $251,184. Who gets that $42,811? Maya does, again only after she sells or refinances her property. So she is seeing another 6.8% p.a. return.

Unfortunately, all these types of returns are not additive but here's what we know so far—

ROE, return on equity	4.1%	per year
Wealth effect	6.8%	Per year
Real estate inflation on property	3.5%	per year
Real estate inflation on equity	11.7%	per year

As you already know, it is my view that the best way to measure financial returns (not just for real estate but for any type of investment) is using the internal rate of return, IRR. For advanced practitioners, I have included an entire section below on how to do this. What the IRR does is blend all these types of returns into a single number. Here is Maya's IRR if she decides to sell her rental property after 5 years—

IRR	**15.3%**	**per year**

Now it is not Ms Yates' intention to sell her property after 5 years. Quite the contrary, she intends to keep all her rental properties and use them to help her provide for her retirement. But IRR calculations require that you bound them, i.e., have an end date.

I like IRRs much more than I do cap rates (which, because they are so easy to calculate, the realtor industry really loves) because the latter ignores wealth effects and real estate inflation. But where time periods are short and real estate inflation is large, IRRs can mask problems like a property that doesn't cashflow each month which means you expect or hope to be bailed out by a selling price that more than catches you up for your monthly losses. As a result, I calculate all these ratios and so should you. One thing I know is: NEVER BUY A PROPERTY THAT DOESN'T CASHFLOW.

You should also know that under certain circumstances IRR calculations can yield two values only one of which is right so you actually have to use judgment. At the end of the day, every decision to invest is an act of faith not just calculation. You improve your odds when your heart, your gut and your brain are all in alignment so performing an analysis like the above is necessary but not sufficient.

It's like getting married—you hope it'll all work out and sometimes, you're disappointed.

Maya's Longterm View

So here's the thing—when Ms Yates is 62 and assuming she still owns her principal residence plus she has three rental properties each like the first one described above, and assuming she has by then paid off all her mortgages, here's what her cashflow from her mini real estate empire looks like—

	Maya's Longterm View	
Principal residence	$676.45	per month
First rental property	$1,799.45	per month
Second rental property	$1,799.45	per month
Third rental property	$1,799.45	per month
Total NOI	$6,074.80	per month
Total NOI	$72,897.60	per year

I encourage people I coach to use leverage in initial stages of building their real estate portfolios and then at some point to stop doing that and focus on paying their mortgages off. Leverage has a way of goosing your returns, the more of it the better to a point. If you use leverage to put together a rental portfolio like the one above, you actually pay off your total mortgage debt faster if, perversely, you have more of it. Huh? Assuming your properties are: 1. in decent locations, 2. you've bought smart (i.e., you didn't pay too much), 3. you have a plan that will make sure to the greatest extent possible that they cashflow, then ROE, cap rate, IRR, NOI, wealth effects and real estate inflation will all work for you producing a fount of money which will allow you to start paying off your mortgages faster than the amortization curves allow because most lenders will allow you at least once per year to take your surplus cashflow (assuming you don't blow it on nice trips to Europe or visiting large amusement parks in Florida and California) and apply it to mortgage balances.

Now Maya's cashflow at age 62 is not quite what she was aiming for—$84,000 per year but, as we saw above, she can expect another $21,528 from social security and her 401(k) and perhaps Badge Amber will still be yielding $900 per month so her retirement income might actually be in the range of $105,200 of which only her real estate portfolio income is truly *inflation protected*. Rents tend to move up over the longterm with inflation so if inflation ever gets back to the 18% p.a. it was in the 1980s, her 401(k) and social security might not be of much help to her. Women like Maya who don't smoke and are careful about their health might well live into their 90s or longer. The fastest growing demographic in many developed nations is 100 up. So they need to plan for a long, long retirement.

Maybe you have a better idea—you know how to find oil in your backyard, win the mega millions lottery or pick the right parent (Warren Buffett would be nice). But Betty Windsor, the

Emperor of Japan, the Holy Roman Catholic Church and nearly two thirds of the richest families in many developed nations have not found (in more than 3,000 years of trying by some really smart people) a better solution than to have most of their wealth invested in real estate. So it's probably right for you and me too.

It is also clear to me that no one is going to rescue you except you. If you expect governments or corporations to provide for you or for that matter you hope your spouse will, you may well be eating bird feed for breakfast and dinner (sorry no lunch, you'll be too poor). And everywhere you look today, it is harder on women than men. Not only do women do about 65% of all work on this planet (in home and out of it combined), they outlive men by 8 years on average. So while maybe Maya can't save $2, $4 or $6 million for her retirement, perhaps she can own her own home and acquire a few rental properties along the way.

(If you would like a copy of Maya's spreadsheet, please download it from here: http://www.old.dramatispersonae.org/images/maya%27s-home.xls.)

Capitalization Rate

Most real estate professionals do not use IRR, Internal Rate of Return—they use cap rates to compare one project with another. The cap rate is an approximate measure, as all financial measures are anyway. It measures only cash-on-cash returns ignoring wealth effects, inflationary trends and the time value of money. Nevertheless, it's a handy first order of magnitude measure. It is especially useful when comparing one opportunity with another. The cap rate is determined by dividing the net operating income of a property by its selling price. This means that, from a buyer's point of view, if you are thinking of buying a residential rental property, one with a 5.5% cap rate is better than one with a 4.5% return. From a seller's point of view, a lower cap rate for the sector or neighborhood implies a higher selling price for you. So the higher the cap rate, the better it is for the buyer and the worse for the seller.

One way to look at the *inverse* of the cap rate is that it is an approximation for the number of years it will take you to earn back your capital. It is widely used in the commercial real estate sector.

Another way to look at the cap rate is that it is a rough measure of the cash return on the entire project—it measures the cash-on-cash return for the overall project not just the equity component (unless you finance 100% of the property with equity).

For a project with financing that is provided by both equity and debt usually in the form of first and second mortgages, we can determine the cap rate this way—

Cap rate = ROR, where ROR is the cash-on-cash rate of return for the entire project.

ROR = (NOI + CRF (i, A) x (Selling Price or Purchase Price–Equity))/Selling Price or Purchase Price, where NOI is Net Operating Income, CRF is the Capital Recovery Factor, i is the cost of borrowing and A is the amortization period. We are assuming here that there is a single (first) mortgage in place.

Thus, Cap Rate = (NOI + CRF (i, A) x (Selling Price – Equity))/Selling Price. Basically, the NOI + CRF (i, A) x (Selling Price – Equity) is the NOI for the project before debt servicing; i.e., with the cost of debt financing added back in.

As the amortization period approaches infinity, CRF = i. This is typical when you have interest only mortgages. Usually, interest only mortgages are second mortgages or seller take back mortgages (where the seller is providing some of the financing to make the deal happen). Investors should be careful with interest only mortgages. These should only be used as a bridge to more conventional financing since, by definition, principal is never paid off. If it remains in place for long periods, it becomes "bad" debt in the sense that it never goes away.

Cap rate = (NOI + i(SP − E))/ SP, for A → infinity.

As equity in a project approaches zero (100% of financing is debt), the cap rate is:

Cap Rate = (NOI + i x SP)/ SP, for E → zero.

But NOI will be zero if E = 0 assuming that the selling price is jacked up to the point where all income is used to support debt. In that case, we have:

Cap rate = (i x SP)/ SP, for E approaching zero and NOI approaching zero or cap rate = i.

What we have done in typical engineering fashion is to look at the boundary conditions for our formula and discovered that under certain circumstances, the cap rate is simply equal to the cost of borrowing. This gives you a first order of approximation for determining a cap rate for a project and explains, in part, why real estate is so sensitive to changes in interest rates.
The higher interest rates are, the higher the cap rate will be and, hence, the lower selling prices will be. The opposite is also true. Obviously, Buyers want to purchase property with the highest possible cap rates and Sellers want to sell using the lowest cap rates possible.
Real estate is highly cyclic and moves largely with interest rates. As we found out above, higher cap rates imply lower selling prices but, by definition, it also means lower purchase prices.
Cap rates vary a lot—over time, from city to city, within a city and between sectors—residential cap rates tend to be lower than, say, commercial cap rates because the former are more sought after by more investors than the latter. The perception is that residential real estate is less risky than commercial real estate and people often don't think they can purchase commercial real estate suspecting that it is either too big or too complex for them. But in many cases, one form of commercial real estate is often open to small investors—industrial buildings and industrial condos can be in a price range reachable for many retail investors. Industrial property can sometimes be less risky to purchase than residential buildings because cap rates are higher, cashflows better, leases longer and not subject to rent control plus there's the fact that competition to buy this type of property is usually less.
Do you want to make money in real estate? Then buy when everybody else is selling (i.e., when cap rates are highest and interest rates are highest) and sell when everyone else is buying (i.e., when cap rates are lowest and interest rates are lowest). A simpler way to put it is, "Buy low, sell high."
Now this is easier said than done. As discussed above, people are very sheep like. We like to buy what and when everyone else is buying. Ever bought a suit or dress and had the salesperson tell you, "This is really *in* this season—everyone who is anyone is buying this." They tell you this because it works.
It's hard to buy real estate when no one else is and interest rates are high. Everyone will tell you not to—your CFO, your auditor, your bank, your spouse, your BOD (Board of Directors), your CAO, COO, your lawyer, even your CTO (Chief Techie) will not want you to—she or he will want more funding for their department instead—it'll have a better ROR, or so they will tell you. But you are the CEO and, at the end of the day, the decision is yours.

The best deals I ever did were when real estate markets were depressed. I bought some land near a major shopping centre in 1983 when interest rates were 18-19%. The land cost me $1 per square foot for ten acres. In 1984, I got an offer for the property at 50 cents per square foot—I thought I was in real trouble. But I went to my dad and he reminded me about rule number 1—buy low/sell high so I declined the offer.

By 1985/86, interest rates were down by half and I sold four acres for $10 per square foot to an auto dealer and the other six acres to an industrial company for $12. We made about $4m in three years on an investment of $450k; you don't need to bother doing an IRR calculation or figure out what your ROI or ROE on deals like this is—they are good deals.

By 1994, the real estate business was again in a slump. These up and down cycles seem to have a frequency of about seven years. Real estate tends to *lead* the national economy into a recession and lag it coming out which means it usually lasts longer than a general recession. But when real estate bounces, it rebounds in a hurry so you have to start selling right away if you want to time the market. In 1994, I bought 60 acres of industrial land in a suburban location for just 15 cents a square foot. I couldn't believe it—people were just giving the stuff away—prices were lower than at any time since the great Depression of the 1930s. By 1999, a tech boom had pushed land in the area up to $6 then $8 per square foot. Buyers were plentiful and land wasn't.

Think about that, land went from 15 cents per square foot to $8 in just five or six years. It's an industry where patient, anti-cyclical investors can make money without being geniuses.

Going back to the 1980s once more, a good friend of mine (Bill) asked me what I was going to do. I told him I was planning on building office buildings and shopping plazas. At the time, office rents were about $18 per square foot per year triple net. "Triple net" means net of operating costs, property taxes and utilities. The year was 1983.

I asked Billy what he was going to do. He said buy land and develop his portfolio for parking lots until a better use comes along. I thought, 'How boring.' But parking fees in that city went from $25 per month in 1983 to $85 by 1989 to $125 in the 1990s and $225 today. This works out to a compounded growth rate of 7.6% p.a. in parking prices over that period, much better than office rents which went from $18 per sf (square foot) in 1983 to $6 just six years later. Meanwhile land prices downtown in the same city increased nearly as much—by a factor of 7 as compared to 9 for parking fees. So Billy today has a lovely home in Palm Beach, a flat in London, another one in Monaco while yours truly works for a living selling real estate and writing about it. He flies into the city only for as long as it takes to collect another huge check for selling one of his paring lots to a developer for yet another residential condo tower. And, I should point out, parking lots are an easier business to run than, say, siting, designing, financing, building, leasing and maintaining office structures.

A client of mine bought an industrial building for his moving and packing supplies business. He believes in owning his own real estate both for a family home and for his company. He bought the SDPC building sold for $4.8m. His company occupies about half the premises and the other half he rents out. The cap rate for his acquisition is:

Cap Rate (SDPC) = (NOI + CRF(i, A) x (SP − E))/ $4,800,000 = ($301,736 + $313,864)/ $4,800,000 = 12.825%

From his point of view (as the buyer), this looks good. Cap rates for industrial property can easily be in the 9, 10, 11 or 12% range which means a lower cost of acquisition for Paul (not his real name).

As discussed above, another way to use the cap rate is to calculate its inverse which gives you a rough measure of how long it takes to get your money back. Another useful engineering trick is to check your units, viz:

Inverse of cap rate units = $/($/yr + $/yr) = $/$/yr = yr

So Paul's new project takes 7.8 years to return all of the capital back to Paul (his equity) *and* to his debt holders. That is pretty fast if you think about the average homeowner taking 20, 25 or 30 years to pay off their home mortgage which many actually never accomplish.

But Paul should be much more interested in when he gets his equity back—this means he can turn around and do something else with it—buy more real estate, buy more equipment for his packing supplies business, go on a nice holiday, buy a boat, whatever.

You get an approximate time for Paul to get his money back by simply dividing his Equity by the NOI. This works out to $1.2m divided by $301,736 or roughly 4 years. The IRR is a much more precise tool but it seems that the industry is just much more comfortable with a 'rule of thumb' cap rate approach.

Now let's look at the cap rate for a small investment property. Let's use as an example, a multi-residential building, "Langlier Place" which has 12, 1-bedroom units and 36, 2-bedroom units. Note that it is important to know whether the cap rates you are using are effectively net or gross cap rates. The cap rates calculated above used gross operating income; for small investment properties you typically use net operating income where NOI is found by subtracting operating costs that the owner must pay from revenues received. Operating costs do not include either depreciation or mortgage interest. This is because cap rates remove from their calculation the debt structure of the existing or previous owner. Obviously, a large well funded REIT, pen fund or insurance company will have a lower COF (cost of funds) than a typical private investor.

Therefore, for cap rates to be useful to compare one property with another similar one (similar in terms of quality, location, age, etc.), you need to remove the impact of different capital structures.

Langlier Place—Owner's Pro Forma v Langlier Place—Appraiser's Pro Forma

Revenues

YEAR 1 YEAR 2 YEAR 3
Rent $688,000 $694,000 $698,000
Parking and Laundry $ 24,000 $ 24,800 $ 26,400
Total $712,000 $718,800 $724,400
Expenses
Realty taxes.. $ 52,800
Water... $ 9,800
Hydro... nil*
Insurance... $ 7,800
Maintenance and Repairs...................................... $ 5,500
Painting.. $12,000
Supplies... $ 1,300
Elevator maintenance.. $ 1,100
Accounting and Legal.. $ 3,000
Superintendent.. $ 22,000

Mortgage Payments** (Principal and Interest).........	$404,186
Total Operating Costs...	$519,486

Potential Gross Income

12, 1-bedroom units @ market rent of $900 each.........	$129,600
36, 2-bedroom units @ market rent of $1,325 each.......	$572,400
Sub-total...	$702,000

Additional Income

Parking, 42 spaces @ $55 per month............................	$ 27,720
Laundry, 5 w/d @ $30 per month.................................	$ 1,800
Total Potential Gross Income......................................	$731,520
Less vacancy allowance of 6%.....................................	-$ 43,912
Effective Gross Income..	$687,628

Operating Costs

Realty taxes..	$ 52,800
Water..	$ 9,800
Hydro..	nil*
Insurance...	$ 7,800
Maintenance and Repairs...	$ 5,500
Painting...	$12,000
Supplies...	$ 1,300
Elevator maintenance..	$ 1,100
Accounting and Legal...	$ 3,000
Superintendent..	$ 22,000
Property Management (3% of Effective Gross Income)............	$ 20,629
Total Operating Costs..	$135,929
Net Operating Income..	$204,914
Semi-Net Annual Operating Income..............................	$551,699
Selling Price..	$6,500,000
Cap Rate...	8.49%

(* Paid by Tenants.)

(** Mortgage is a Canadian mortgage of $4.2 million with an interest rate of 7.25% and amortization period of 20 years.)

You will notice that the cap rate for Langlier Place is calculated using a 'semi-net' operating income. This shows how difficult seat-of-the-pants cap rates can be. As long as you know how the cap rate you are being quoted was arrived at, it can be a useful way to compare one property with another. But what if someone is using NOI and someone else is using a semi-net number and someone else is using gross income? Cap rates require care in their use.

Internal Rate of Return

Probably the truest measure of a project's rate of return is its Internal Rate of Return. The IRR is that interest rate that exactly balances the discounted value of future net cashflows with the investment required to develop the project or enterprise. The higher the interest rate (discount rate) needs to be in order that future net cashflows exactly offset upfront investment, the higher the IRR is and the better the project is, at least in terms of return on investment.

The IRR can be found by solving the following equation by trial and error (computers do it using an iterative process).

Equation to Determine IRR

In the simplest model, if a student loans a professor $1,000 and the professor pays it back in three years with interest of, say, $150 per year, we have:

Year Investment/Cashflow (from the student's POV)
0 -$1,000
1 $150
2 $150
3 $1,150

The IRR can be found by solving the following equation by trial and error (not much trial or error here):

$-\$1{,}000 + \$150/(1+irr)^1 + \$150/(1+irr)^2 + \$1{,}150/(1+irr)^3 = 0$ or IRR = 15% p.a.

Now, I have done survey after survey (not scientifically, I may add) of my students over the years and I haven't yet found many students willing to lend their (poor) professor $1,000 in return for $150 per year of interest. They usually aren't interested until the money gets to be around $200 a year and most of them are looking for even more, $300 or $400 in interest per year. This implies that their personal discount rates (Internal Rates of Return) are in the 20 to 40% p.a. range.

Some work I did earlier on rates of return for students pursuing an architecture degree suggested that their personal IRRs are in the range of just 14%*. There could be a number of factors at work here including the possibility that architects (unlike more hard headed engineers like me or business students) are somewhat "other directed' (a nice way of saying they are taking their architecture degrees for reasons other than acquiring big bucks).

(* Please see: A Case Study of the Perceived Value of An Architecture Degree, Carleton University, Ottawa, Canada, http://www.eqjournal.org/?p=1061.)

In any event, it is well known that personal discount rates tend to fall as people get older because: a. they have usually have more money as they get older and a greater supply of money implies that its price will fall, and b. their willingness to take risks drops so that they would rather have it in t-bills or CDs than startups by the time most people are in their 50s, 60s, 70s or 80s.

IRR AS A FUNCTION OF AGE AND CORPORATE SIZE
Personal Discount Rates Vary with Age

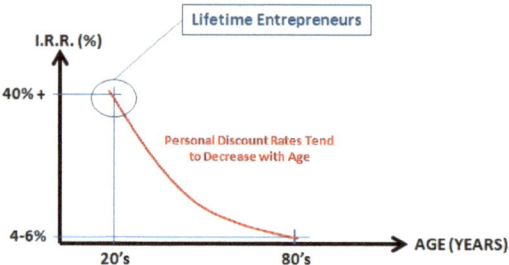

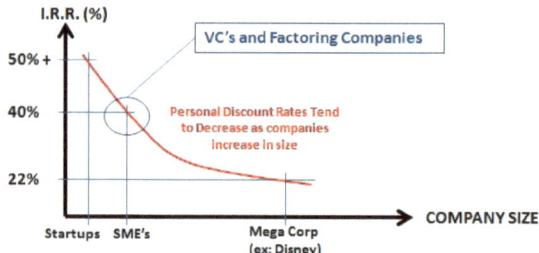

Personal Discount Rates Vary with Age

Just as IRRs tend to decrease with age, they tend to drop as companies become larger. Mega corporations tend to have minimum expectations for their IRRs (on their equity) of around 20 to 22% p.a. Entrepreneurs and startups usually require much higher IRRs than this because so many things can and do go wrong that they have to aim high just so they don't go oob (out of business).

When the Disney Company acquired an expansion franchise in the NHL in the early 1990s, there was some concern that Disney could afford to "buy" players and push up salaries even faster than they were already going up. Executives from that company including its then CEO (Mike Eisner) reassured NHL Expansion Committee members that every Disney investment including sports teams had to meet certain minimum investment criteria and this shouldn't be a concern. The Mighty Ducks of Anaheim (now the Ducks) began play within a couple of years thereafter and Mike was true to his word.

If you download the spreadsheet for a (rental) homebuilder posted at: http://www.old.dramatispersonae.org/IRR/SampleIRR2.xls, you will see that if an investor/builder/developer puts down, say, 25% equity on each unit, he or she will see a 22% p.a. IRR. But if they put down just 5%, the IRR on their equity jumps to 56% p.a. In both cases, the IRR of the project hasn't changed—it remains 10.8%. What this tells you is that the IRR for a project (or enterprise) is made up of a series of IRRs on equity and debt. In this case, the capital structure is simple—there are just two components: the investor/builder/developer's equity and the bank's or lender's mortgage debt.

So the IRR for the project (10.8%) is like a 'weighted' average of the IRR on equity (22%, or 56% in the case using greater leverage) and the IRR on debt (which equals the interest rate on the mortgage, i.e., 6%). For more complex projects, you can have many components in the capital structure—equity, structured equity, debenture debt, secured debt, sub debt, capital lease, unsecured debt and so forth. Each tranche will have its own cashflow profile and IRR.

You might ask how lenders can afford to lend money at 6% when the above graph suggests that large corporations want minimum IRRs of 20 to 22% p.a. on their equity? Well, just ask yourself how much interest you are getting on your savings account. If the answer is less than 1% (in fact, after you calculate all the fees you pay your bank, it is probably negative), then you can figure it out for yourself. Bottom line, lenders like banks use OPM (Other People's Money) mixed in with a little of their own so that their IRRs on their equity are among the best on the planet. Don't worry about your bank's rate of return, worry about your own.

(More recently, I added a similar spreadsheet for an investor or sitting owner (owner occupier) of industrial condos. See: http://www.old.dramatispersonae.org/IRR/SampleIRR2-commercial.xls.)

Again, I did two cases: one where you buy/invest in one industrial condo with 25% down and a second case where you buy five units with 5% down. In all probability, in the commercial space, you might more realistically do a case where you buy one with 40% down or two with 20% down since LTV (Loan to Value) ratios tend to be lower than in the residential sector.

Still the principle is the same: more leverage increases your return on equity under certain conditions. Your total return is again made up of three components: cash on cash return (money you make every month assuming your mortgage and other payments are less than your rents), inflation (all inflation in real estate values go to the equity owner assuming your local marketplace is not going through a recession) and forced savings (paydown of mortgage either by sitting owner or tenants).

Establishing Sales Goals Using a Reverse IRR Model

A reverse IRR model* helps you establish monthly goals for your new enterprise that, if (when) achieved, will allow you to pay your bills and make a profit too. You want to make a profit not only so you can take nice holidays but also so you can reinvest in your business in terms of adopting new technology, creating new products or new services, adding more personnel, doing more staff training and so forth.

(* You can download this model from:
http://www.old.dramatispersonae.org/IRR/ReverseIRRAcmePromotions.xls.)

People are really good at reaching goals once they set them. If you are involved in a timed race, you always want to go second or nearer to the end when you will know what your key competitors' times are. Then you have a goal which you can break down into intervals and beat.

Same thing for business. It does you no good to say, I want $150k in sales my first year. What you need to say is, I need $12,500 a month in sales or $625 a day, every day for the 20 working days in each month.

Visualization is key. Put up a sign "N = ?" in your office and at home and every day focus on it and drive N up. (N can be sales, number of customers, number of products shipped, whatever. It is the basic metric for your business.)

Don't think that, oh well, I didn't make $625 in sales today, I'll make it up at month's end. It doesn't work that way. If you miss today's target, it means you have to sell $1,300 tomorrow or $1,925 the day after and pretty soon, you and your business are toast. Enterprises that set goals and track their metrics are growing at *seven* times the rate of enterprises that don't according to a Silicon Valley study published in May of 2011 called *Startup Genome Report 01* by Max Marmer, Bjoern Lasse Herrmann, Ron Berman*. I have found that people who have mentors or coaches who help them set goals and then hold them accountable for their performance do better than those without a support group.

(* http://www.eqjournal.org/Startup_Genome_Report.pdf)

The reverse IRR model is based on the assumption that, going in, you are more likely to know your costs accurately that what your revenues will be. Revenue estimates, whether based on market surveys you did or a guesstimate you came up with as to what percentage of the total market you think you are going to get, can be highly unreliable. So goal setting based on what your expected costs will be plus an allowance for profitability based on some type of target you have established, is probably as good a mechanism to establish your future revenue stream as any.

The Power of Leverage/Using Other People's Money

The power of using OPM (Other People's Money) or leverage (aka debt) is immense. It increases the IRR on your equity and it allows you to ration your use of a limited amount of capital to do more of whatever it is you are planning on doing.

"Compound interest is the eighth wonder of the world.
He who understands it, earns it... he who doesn't... pays it," Albert Einstein

Leverage is usually interpreted (especially by lenders) as increasing risk but as you can see in the rental home example we used above, it may be that if you develop five rental units instead of one, your risks (and your lender's exposure to you as well) may go down not up despite higher gearing.

Archimedes Understood the Power of Leverage

If you use your equity to build five units instead of one (i.e., you are putting 5% down on each unit instead of 25% and financing the rest), and if one tenant leaves, you will have a 20%

vacancy rate instead of 100%. The free cashflow you are earning from the other four (still occupied) units can assist you in paying the mortgage for the vacant fifth unit.

If the average vacancy rate for each unit over a ten year period is, say, 10%, then the probability that all five units would be vacant at the same time is pretty low (0.1 to the power of five or just .001%). So, as entrepreneurs, we can argue (with our lenders) for more leverage not less.

Obviously, they might say:

1. With higher levels of equity, there is a better (from the lender's point of view) debt to equity ratio which means if asset values tumble, their loans are protected by your equity since in a bankruptcy, foreclosure or power of sale proceeding, the secured creditor (the lender) gets paid first. Lenders are not only entitled to get their capital back but also all back interest as well as all legal and accounting fees plus other costs they incur in terms of enforcing their security.

2. If you only had one unit instead of five and it becomes vacant, your income from other sources might be enough to cover your loan payments* but if you had to cope with all five units suddenly becoming vacant, you could be under water in a hurry.

(* This is known as cashflow coverage for your loan; i.e., your free cashflow as calculated by the lender must be significantly greater than your monthly mortgage obligations or they won't make the loan. Most lenders will usually only include half the rental income you are receiving and will deduct from your employment and other income, your other monthly obligations like home mortgage, car payments, credit card payments, student loans, etc.)

This is what I like to call the 'nuclear bomb scenario' or what other people call a lender's 'belt and suspenders' approach to lending. Banks generally only like to lend money to people who don't need it (i.e., people who have enough of their own cash to start a project without any loans).

From *your* POV, your cash-on-cash returns are much higher if you build five units. The spreadsheet shows if you leverage your $37,500 in equity into five rental properties (with 5% down on each unit), you have a cash return of $254,052.85 over five years as compared to $89,291.00 if you can only build one unit (with a down payment of 25%).

So leverage has the strange effect of being more risky (at least from the lender's POV) but ultimately lets you pay off all your debt obligations much faster than if you used less leverage; i.e., bought only one rental property.

Bottom line, you need a sophisticated, motivated lender before you can do highly leveraged deals.

Your Team

If you want to be successful in real estate, you need a good team around you, one you can trust and who are really good at what they do.

Your team should include: a deal-making attorney, a residential realtor who knows what s/he is doing, a commercial realtor (same thing), a mortgage broker who gets deals done, a creative interior designer, a talented group of contractors/renovators/handypersons, a competent property manager (if you are not doing it yourself), an accurate surveyor, fair appraiser, thorough home or building inspector (who can not only tell you what's wrong with a property but also how to fix it and how much it will cost), willing bank and other secondary lenders, knowledgeable engineering/environmental/soils consultants, no nonsense urban planner, effective lobbyist, title insurance/mortgage insurance/building and property insurance/life insurance providers, a coach/mentor who assists you in terms of setting goals and achieving them, creative home stager and artful landscaper who helps you not only maintain the outdoor space but improve it, accountant with knowledge of the real estate industry assists you to be tax efficient and get your holdings structured properly.

You will also need good relationships with suppliers for building materials and appliances as well as with your city's buildings and plans departments so when you need something from them (like a building permit, a license, an occupancy permit or an inspection), you get them on a timely basis.

Value Proposition of a Residential Realtor

I work in the real estate brokerage industry and I am amazed at how poorly most of the industry is at explaining their value proposition. The FSBO (For Sale by Owner) market is growing and REALTORS in Canada and the US are losing ground. Now I realize I am biased because of the work I do, but surely residential REALTORS (and commercial ones too—but that is a subject I deal with elsewhere) can do a better job of explaining what it is they do and how they add value to a transaction.

Clients often fail to understand what REALTORS actually do for them. Now whose fault is that? I would say it's the REALTOR industry's fault for not clearly explaining their value proposition. Of all the professionals involved in a typical residential or commercial real estate transaction, they all get paid by the hour except REALTORs (and possibly mortgage brokers) who only get paid (usually) on successful completion of an Agreement of Purchase and Sale. This might explain why so many lawyers are of the deal breaking kind instead of the deal making type—the more issues they can find, the more hours they can bill for. But it doesn't explain why they tend to do nothing unless asked to by their clients. They sit and wait for "instructions".

REALTORs can't afford to do that.

In my view, most residential REALTORs do a great job. I can say this because I do mostly commercial work and I must say I admire the stick-to-it'ness of most of these residential folks. They work seven days a week (most showings are on weekends and evenings), they are always on call (their clients want 15 minute or less response time so they are tethered to their smart phones*), they drive clients they don't know much about around showing them two dozen homes only to find out that: a) they are not qualified to buy (maybe they exaggerated their ability to purchase) or b) they find something on their own (despite sometimes having signed a buyer agency agreement tying them to their sales representative) and put the transaction through the listing agency (not realizing that the listing agency is now a dual agent representing both Seller and Buyer and not necessarily looking out for the Buyer's best interest).

(* A residential REALTOR helping me out on a commercial transaction answered his cell phone on a Saturday night while sitting around a camp fire after the deal blew up and we needed to speak with him urgently. I said, "George, you are amazing. No commercial sales rep I know would answer his phone at this time. I salute you." I couldn't believe his dedication.)

Here is another example. I was at an NHL game and with five minutes to go in a tight game, one of my buddies got up to leave. "Mike, where you going? The game's not over."

"I have a client who wants to meet me at 10:00 pm to make a counter offer on the home they are buying. Got to go, thanks for the game…"

Now that is dedication. Residential REALTORS are out there at night in freezing weather doing deals and servicing their clients.

Commercial people like me have it much easier—our clients get in early but by 5 or 6 pm, that's it, they go home and they don't want to hear from you evenings and weekends unless it is REALLY urgent.

Now residential REALTORS aren't just heroes because they brave cold weather, waste their gas on clients who are not really serious or get left at the altar by clients who ditch them at the last minute. They add real dollars and cents to transactions.

Here are some of the ways they do that:

1. A decent residential REALTOR does dozens of agreements per year. The FSBO usually does only one, two or three in a lifetime. As a result, the residential REALTOR is, in all likelihood, going to have a much higher level of expertise in terms of negotiating and completing these transactions. Most people don't know that REALTORS are required in many jurisdictions to take six quite difficult courses and exams to become fully licensed and, if they want to become brokers, they must do additional study and examinations. They must get 75% or better to pass and their regulators are completely inflexible on this. Then, every two years they need to do 24 additional credits. In another generation, REALTORS will go from being a second career to being a first choice career and a profession and maybe even a calling. I realize the latter sounds corny but I certainly enjoy working with clients and I feel good when a client buys his or her own building for their company and they walk in and they have realized their dream to own their own real estate…

(* Some of my very smart university students are taking their real estate licenses. Some are scraping through with 75s and 76s. Some are failing with 73s. So the courses are non-trivial and, in my view, actually quite good.)

2. If the FSBO fails to sell his or her property and then enlists an agency, the likely selling price may be lower because the listing has become "tired" or "stigmatized".

3. The agency has access to MLS data (which helps set list prices) and usually has a list of established buyers. More than half of all residential real estate transactions are derived directly or indirectly from existing clients.

4. The chances of not completing a FSBO agreement are also much higher. Real estate transactions are the only area of commerce that I know about where, by law, the agreement in most jurisdictions must be in writing. I guess because of the importance for most people of the sale of their home, these transactions are required to be written agreements. Real estate is tricky and a lot can go wrong*. Reducing the probability of failure significantly increases the value brought by the REALTOR to a transaction.

(* The list of what can go wrong is endless—conditions waived before building inspections or financings are completed; chattels or fixtures that are thought to be included that aren't; lawyers who don't get paperwork done on time to complete deals. How about an Oklahoma offer? Ever heard of those? The term comes from the Dust Bowl of the 1930s in that state where some smart Yankees fleeced naïve Okies out of their farms. Suppose you get an offer on your home from a nice young couple that you think are terrific. You are a FSBO and they need a "bit of help". Will you give them a second mortgage for just a couple of years so they can buy your home? 'Sure, why not,' you think. So you sell your home to them for $300,000 with a $75,000 seller take back mortgage with interest at 8%, interest only paid monthly in arrears. But what you don't know is that you have to specify what is the maximum first mortgage they are allowed to place on your property. You didn't know that. So on completion, you find that they have arranged a 95% first mortgage which together with their second mortgage (from you) means they have $360,000 cash on hand to buy your $300,000 home; thus, they have an extra $60,000 in their jeans on closing. If they default, you can repo (repossess) your house (by foreclosure or power of sale) but you have to deal with the fact that the mortgages on the property are now worth more than the home's market value. God forbid that they used it for a grow op too. Many grow op homes have to be condemned because of the uncontrolled spread of mold due to high humidity levels in the house. Anyway, this is how sleazy con men defrauded many innocent Okies out of their farms and walked away with huge fortunes from the misfortune of the hardest hit folks during the Great Depression. Using a professional realtor can help.)

5. Legal disputes are also a costly reality. For example, if there are certain fixtures or chattels or outbuildings in dispute, this can further increase the value of the realtor's services by avoiding costly litigation. Realtors are required to be insured in most places to provide Sellers and Buyers with additional protection. The FSBO is not insured against legal risk. What if a FSBO takes a deposit and the conditions in the transaction are not fulfilled? Will the FSBO return the deposit? In the case of realtors, the deposits are held in trust accounts, which also happen to be insured.

6. Legal fees for FSBO transactions may be higher as lawyers attempt to fix mistakes made by inexperienced Buyers and Sellers.

7. The benefits of agency are likely to be higher for higher priced homes.

8. The agency also brings other services: for instance, experts on home staging that cost as little as $300 but can add significantly to the value of a home. Other experts such as home inspectors, home appraisers or mortgage brokers can also be brought into a transaction.

9. One other item needs to be mentioned and that is the value of a person's time. It takes time to gain the expertise of a realtor and also it takes time to sell a home: to list it, to put it on MLS, to show it, to draw up the agreement, to arrange for inspections and financing, to waive conditions, to provide lawyers with documents, etc. If a person's time is worth $20 per hour or $100 per hour, you have a significant saving for homeowners who use realtors. Homeowners are often better off using their time more productively in the things that they do to make a living rather than trying to be realtors.

10. The agency saves the FSBO her or his marketing costs and costs to join a FOR-SALE-BY-OWNER network.

11. The agency will do open houses, showings and negotiations. It is not easy representing yourself and many people find it especially difficult to tout their own horns…

12. Now when people hear that a home is *For Sale By Owner*, they immediately discount the price by 5% (because the client is not "paying a commission") then take a bit more off so that they have some negotiating room.

13. Buyers will often not feel comfortable representing themselves, so while they may show up to look by themselves, when it comes time to present an offer, they will engage a buyer rep to do that for them.

14. Of course, a buyer rep may ask the Seller if they will pay a commission but perhaps ask for 2.5% instead of 5% because they are representing the Buyer and giving what is known in the trade as "customer" service to the Seller.

15. The Seller figures they are still coming out ahead by "saving" 2.5% of the sale price but they could be fooling themselves—they could actually be paying the full commission and more because the price offered is more than 5% below what they would have otherwise received because of the strategy employed by the Buyer and their buyer agent.

16. Not only can they end up with less money from the transaction than if they had used a listing agency, they are doing all the work and taking all the risks.

17. It may also take longer to sell your home if you go the FSBO route. If you are changing jobs, moving cities, need the money, whatever, that extra time to sell could place quite a burden on you.

18. Lastly, people are highly emotional. I have seen negotiations come to an end because a Seller and Buyer couldn't come to agreement on who pays utility costs for the day of closing (normally, it is the Seller). On a $350,000 transaction, we are talking about a dispute over perhaps $10.

Humans have two amygdalae which modulate our reactions to events and warn us of peril. They are essential to our ability to feel emotion (including fear) and to perceive them in other people. They control how we react to the presence of reward, sexual partners, rivals, children in trouble, danger, and so forth. They form an older part of the brain and have many connections with other structures. They are powerful parts of the human mind and drive a lot of behaviors, many of them negative ones.

Angry people lose ten points off their IQ and do things that are often against their own best interests. Realtors and other professional negotiators like arbitrators and conciliators can often insulate Buyers and Sellers from their own worst instincts.

Deal Makers

Trained negotiators don't use terms like:

"take it or leave it",
"that's my final offer",
"I guarantee it",
"are you blind/deaf?",
"that's a stupid question",
"that'll never happen",
"I've got a backup offer",
"that's confidential",
"make me an offer",
"everything's for sale at a price",
"I'm all-in",
"you're a loser",
"I'm all about big win for me, little win for you",
"I'm dealing your cards face-up",
"you're a liar",
"I need to call my lawyer",
"you're making a mountain out of a molehill",
"that's non negotiable",
"I'm going to sue you" or "see you in court",
"that's undiscussable",
"I'm the expert",
"pretend I'm a call girl—I want to be paid upfront",
"that's blackmail" or "is that a threat?",
"cry me a river",
"I'm not paying for that" or "don't cheap out on me",
"I'm bluffing",
"I'd bet my life on it",
"let me see your cards before I bet",
"talk is cheap",
"I'm too busy",
"I don't care",
"I've made you an offer, you can't refuse",
"let's continue these negotiations in the bar".

I am sure you have heard the one about the lawyer (or doctor) who represents (treats) himself. S/he has a client who is a fool.

I have summarized the value proposition of a residential realtor on a spreadsheet. You can download it in .xls format. Here is the URL:

http://www.old.dramatispersonae.org/images/ValuePropositionFSBOVersusAgency.xls.

I estimate that for the sale of a $315,000 home, the agency will receive a commission of around $15,435 but the agency is adding a total of around $38,000 in value to this transaction. So if my calculations are right, the FSBO is better off to enlist the services of a good quality realtor to the tune of approximately $23,000. The spreadsheet shows the assumptions I used to get there. You can fool around with the variables—higher selling prices, lower selling prices, higher or lower commissions, more or less time spent selling a home by a FSBO. The cells are interconnected so one change by you in a key variable will automatically change the bottom line.

Value Proposition of a Commercial REALTOR

The value proposition of engaging a commercial realtor as well as owning your own real estate can be summarized as follows:

1. The agency has access to not only MLS data but usually commercial transaction data bases, as well as a list of established Buyers and Sellers. More than two thirds of all real estate commercial transactions we do at our brokerage are derived either from existing clients' inventory or a desire on their part to add to their portfolios.

2. A commercial realtor like a residential one typically does dozens of agreements per year and develops a facility with these agreements that is unmatched even by most lawyers.

3. The probability of completing an agreement is significantly higher through their involvement. Again, real estate transactions must be, by law, in writing. Real estate is complex and a lot can go wrong. Due diligence is especially important in terms of commercial transactions. You have not only building inspections to worry about but also often examination of leases, completing complex financings, arranging for seller take back mortgages, environmental audits, ensuring that chattels and fixtures are properly accounted for and included, examination of maintenance records, understanding building systems, examination of contracts and sub-contracts for property management and maintenance, reviewing rental equipment agreements, doing appraisals, providing law firms with the paperwork to complete deals on time, checking zoning ordinances... For a more complete list of due diligence, see the appendix at the end of this book.

4. Legal disputes are also a costly reality. Sellers often make representations about things like NOI which turn out, to be kind, to be hyperbole. It is much better to discover that net operating income is much lower than what is shown during a due diligence period than after you complete a transaction. At that point, you can get out of the deal (by not waiving or fulfilling your condition) or ask for a price abatement. After you close, your only alternative is likely to be expensive, time sucking, soul destroying litigation.

5. The agency brings a sense of what the market is doing at any given time. CMA (comparative market analysis) gives Buyers the confidence that they are entering into a sound arrangement.

6. Spreadsheets that estimate the Internal Rate of Return (IRR) for a project are one of the key decision tools that a Buyer needs to have. The IRR takes into account the three types of returns that real estate provides: cash on cash returns, forced savings (the pay down of mortgage principal each month) and real estate inflation. Your commercial realtor should be able to assist you with that.

7. Additionally, there are potential financial advantages of owning real estate including sheltering of income using depreciation reserves. Your realtor and a competent accountant with real estate expertise should be able to help you structure your affairs to be more tax efficient.

8. It takes time to gain the expertise of a realtor and also it takes time to sell or buy property especially commercial real estate. Commercial clients, like residential ones, are often better off using their time more productively in the things that they do to make a living rather than trying to become realtors.

9. Agencies do most of the negotiating. Many Buyers do not feel comfortable representing themselves. Even though most business people think they are logical, the fact is they are not. We often act against our own best interests. Realtors can hold up a mirror and act as a filter so (negotiation killing) comments like the ones I quoted above get left where they belong—unsaid.

10. It may also take longer to source or sell a property, negotiate an agreement and complete it if you go without representation.

11. Owning your own real estate can alleviate future rental increases, provide for security of tenure, allow the owner to develop brand equity in a location that they retain over long periods of time, diversify their asset mix, provide for their retirement, make an operating business more sellable and/or provide for a hierarchy and diversity of ownership that makes tax sense and operating sense.

12. Real estate values are quite stable in most cities over time—it is get rich, slow.

13. It can be less expensive to own than to rent.

14. Owning your own real estate gives you more financial flexibility too—if there is a sudden need for cash, you can re-mortgage your property to access that.

15. Interest rates are hitting historic lows and prices have come off their peaks in North America. You make money in real estate when you buy not when you sell.

Why Use Mortgage Brokers?

In an email exchange with one of my former students, I summarized some of the advantages that mortgage brokers bring to the table:

1. They can source mortgages from 8, 10, 12 or more lenders and get the most competitive interest rate and terms for you to select from.
2. It saves you a lot of time. How long would it take you to get in front of and apply to, say, a dozen lenders?
3. Banks sometimes try to sell tied products—property insurance, mortgage insurance, life insurance, car insurance, mutual funds, other banking services, credit cards and more, "forcing" you to buy things along with your new mortgage that: a) you don't need and b) at higher prices than you can get elsewhere. Mortgage insurance is one of those. You are almost always better off buying life or term insurance from an independent provider than taking your bank's or lender's mortgage insurance.
4. Mortgage brokers can source multiple lenders with one credit report on you and your partner. If you apply to multiple lenders yourself, each one will "ping" your credit rating and each ping on your credit rating lowers your Beacon Score (your credit rating) by 2.7 points. Thus, if you apply separately to 12 lenders, you would lower your credit score by 32.4 points. If your Beacon Score was just above 700 (a good score) before, it would now be below 700 and this could affect your loan rate (i.e., if the interest rate goes up because your credit score has gone down, your mortgage just got more expensive.) The theory is that your credit score goes down since, as far as a credit bureau is concerned, you are applying "all over town" for more and more credit. This is, of course, unfair because you are only applying for one mortgage of, say, $200,000, but it appears to be multiple applications for $2.4 million in financing and, hence, your credit score drops.
5. It usually doesn't cost you a thing. Mortgage lenders, especially in residential real estate, usually pay the mortgage broker a fee for sourcing a loan. These fees are fairly small (anywhere between .75% and .85%, occasionally rising to as much as 1% of loan amount). If lenders don't pay it to independent mortgage brokers, they would have paid it anyway to

their internal people who source mortgages for them. So it really does cost you nothing extra. With commercial mortgages, borrowers often pay a fee as well.

6. It isn't just the interest rate that you need to be concerned about. Many people are doing debt consolidations and need higher loan amounts and better terms and amortization schedules. Your mortgage broker can get you that because lenders know they are competing for the business. Any bank that tells you that because you are a loyal customer and have been with them for a long time, you don't need to shop around and that they will give you the best deal anyway is probably not being straightforward with you.

Here is a spreadsheet I created in .xls format that tries to quantify the merits of using a residential mortgage broker:
http://www.old.dramatispersonae.org/images/ValuePropositionOfAResidentialMortgageBroker.xls.

More than 75% of all mortgage loans in the US are now sourced through mortgage brokers. The rate in Canada is about 30% but I expect it will increase a lot in the next decade.

When people run short of cash or find they are paying out a lot out every month and feel like they are never going to get ahead, they usually take a look at their mortgage and debt situation to see if they can do what three of mortgage agent Dilys Hagerman's clients recently did. Here are those examples—

1. Income of $48,000. Mortgage of $155,000. Credit card debt of $13,000. They paid off their existing mortgage and all their credit card debt by putting in place a new mortgage so that their monthly debt payments are now $1,050 less than it was.

2. Income of $77,000. Mortgage of $165,000. Credit card debt of $41,000. Same deal. Their monthly mortgage payment now is $865 less and all their credit card debt is gone.

3. Income of $133,000. Mortgage of $198,000. Line of credit of $105,000. All of it was renegotiated so that these folks are paying $675 less monthly than they were before with exactly the same debt load.

Dilys says, "Don't be scared by your current mortgage lender (probably your bank) who says you'll have to pay a penalty to get out of your deal. In many cases, with interest rates now so low, it is worth it to pay the penalty to close out early. A renewal offer from your current mortgage holder will often come quite close to your renewal date so it makes it difficult for you to then price-shop. It isn't just interest rates you need to be concerned about—you're going to need some flexibility on loan amount and terms too."

Mortgage agent John Walsh had this to say about credit scores—

"Using an actual numerical number for a credit hit can be misleading. As an example, I had one client who tried to get a new car lease. He was consistent. He hit one car lease company every 3-4 weeks. His credit score after 18 months of trying was down to 500 from over 700. He had clean credit otherwise. So he went down roughly 200 points from just 18 hits.

"In this case, he was seen as 'seeking credit'. Someone should have told him what was happening (I did and told him he wouldn't be eligible for a home mortgage for at least another 12 months). He, like so many, had no clue what was happening to his credit.

"A credit score is more of a 'ranking over time'."

Urban versus Suburban

Many cities in North America are intent on densifying their settlement areas not expanding them. It works too, at least if price differentials are any indication of success. In one case study I did, a new 3-bedroom townhome on Centrepointe Drive (located near the inner city) sold for around $401,000. A similar new townhome built by the same company in Morgan's Grant (a western edge suburb) sold for about $230,000. That's a huge $171,000 price gap and the only real difference I could find is that one is closer to the urban core than the other.

It may even be that the suburban townhome is a bit nicer—if having a yard or garden is important to you. The urban town had zero private space. Plus, since it is part of a condo corp and the owner must pay condo fees, the urban town is more expensive on a monthly basis (assuming that the suburban owner values his or her time for lawn maintenance, snow removal, etc at essentially zero.)

So I wondered why someone would pay $171,000 more for basically the same product. I think there is one simple reason: the urban town is (on an as-the-crow-flies basis) just 7.3 klicks from downtown while the suburban town is 20.9 klicks away. Now luckily for this analysis, the two towns were bought by colleagues of mine and they both work at the same place—the urban townhome is located about 6 minutes from their office while the suburban town is about 20 to 25 minutes away. So we have a real-world, paired sample—rare in urban economics and urban design—and the comparative analysis is easy to do with no adjustments required for family size, time, design or location and, thus, highly accurate.

The colleague and his family who live closer save about 500 minutes per week in commuting time compared to the other family living further out. They also save petrol—about 53 liters per month. If we value their time at $45 per hour and gas at 90 cents per liter then the family on Centrepointe Drive is saving (time and gas) worth $16,185 per annum. On the extra investment of $171,000 (the increased price of the urban town), this represents a ROI of (a not-bad) 9.5% p.a. Most of this ROI derives from time savings—gas savings make up just 3.5% of the total.

While the builder's costs are somewhat higher for the urban towns (because of higher land and construction costs), they aren't that much higher—in part, because the closer-in development is being built at a higher density. In other words, the developer is getting a higher yield of towns on their land on Centrepointe Drive which offsets some of their higher costs. So most of the price differential they are getting for their urban towns is probably going to their bottom line. This is good for the developer but is it good for the overall city?

I would argue that higher land prices in the urban core is the right signal to send to the marketplace—it supports the goal of higher density since developers will act rationally to increase their yield on more expensive land. From the homeowner's point of view, they are clearly prepared to pay more for the benefit of saving time and gas—there are lineups to buy these urban towns. But they too are acting rationally. And both are serving the greater good by looking out for their own best interests, faithfully following Adam Smith's principal of the invisible hand.

When people are prepared to pay this much more for an urban town, a virtuous circle results—developers act in a way that will result in an increase in the supply of the more urban and higher density towns because they command a premium price. There are certainly a lot of teardowns going on inside many inner cities where small-scale builders are buying existing single family homes on larger lots and replacing them with doubles or towns.

But what cities might also want to recognize is that there is still a market for suburban property where people trade longer commutes for lower prices and more space and that isn't wrong either. Cities just needs to get their price signals right and the market will respond...

I posted the spreadsheet I used in .xls format at:

http://www.old.dramatispersonae.org/images/TownhomeAorB.xls where you can download it and fool around with it yourself.

Another way to look at the urban-suburban dichotomy is to view them as different nation-states with their own currencies. The urban housing economy experiences: multiple offers on properties, less choice, higher costs, often fewer park and school amenities, more noise, less room for automobiles, more rapid increases in price year over year and, of course, higher density. The suburban housing sector has: more choices both in terms of the housing product itself and in the public room, more park and school amenities, newer inventory, more space per dollar spent, fewer buyers, less housing inflation, lower density and probably less crime (although vandalism and graffiti may be a significant issue for suburban populations too.)

One can easily see why some families prefer suburban locations, not least because they can buy a lot more bedrooms per dollar spent.

In the above example, $1,000 buys 6.7 square feet of housing in suburbia but just 3.9 square feet in urban locations. Put another way, ONE SUBURBAN DOLLAR, let's call it $1 SUB when exchanged for URBAN currency only gets you $0.57 URB. So moving from the nation-state of suburbia to the nation-state of urban locales can be a difficult move unless you temper your expectations in terms of accepting less space and more crowding, as well as higher prices for your 'weaker dollar'.

Here are my calculations:

Purchase Area Price
$1,000 Price per Sq. Ft. Buys
Suburban Town $230,000 1550 sq. ft. $148.39 per sq. ft. 6.739130435 sq. ft.
Urban Town $401,000 1550 sq. ft. $258.71 per sq. ft. 3.865336658 sq. ft.
Ratio of Price per Sq. Ft. 0.573566085 "Exchange Rate"

Walkability Score Makes a Difference

A lecture given by Windmill Developments' Rodney Wilts on LEED buildings was an eye opener. Mr Wilts talked not just about how the built form as well as heating, ventilation and mechanical/electrical systems need to be improved to make structures more green but how walkability plays an important role in determining outcomes today.

Consumers want to buy locations that have access to the things they need via walking; they don't want a home or apartment where everything requires a car trip. Recall what Maya did with her suburban home—traded it for an inner city location.

Mr Wilts says that one of their suburban projects was less successful despite being a beautiful structure because the location was so isolating. They won't make that mistake again.

Sell-through for places that are less walkable are slower, he says, and they sell for less per square foot so developers have to be more aware of the walk score for their prospective projects. A useful resource for determining walk scores is provided by http://www.walkscore.com/.

Here is the way we score homes and rental property*. You will see that location-based factors are important as is the ability to add value and to buy low.

(* You can download this spreadsheet from our server; it's plug and play, www.old.dramatispersonae.org/images/00-housing-matrix-3.xls).

Housing Investment Guide

Variables
Proximity to schools, elder care

Proximity to shopping, restaurants, coffee, groceries
Proximity to desirable neighborhoods
Proximity to hospital/health care
Proximity to Fitness/Recreation/Park
Proximity to Arts, Entertainment and Culture
Proximity to Air and Rail
In home flats, granny flats, work from home permitted
Rentability
Housing inflation
Walkability Score
Transit Score
Bike Score
Location Score
Ability to add parking
Ability to add in-home flat
Ability to add separate entrance
Ability to add curb appeal/landscaping
Ability to improve interior design
Ability to add bench seat with storage/design flair/cornerstone
Overall brand experience
Ability to buy low
Total score

Sub-Prime Blame

People have been blaming the international recession that began in 2008/09 on 'the sub-prime mess'. But whoa, hold them horses a minute; a sub-prime borrower could be your son or daughter, your mother-in-law, your best friend or you and me.

Let's first remember why we have a sub-prime lending market in the first place—it is to make more of our citizens, homeowners. There is the idea that homeowners make better citizens because—

1. They have bought-in to social norms and have a stake in their societies.
2. They benefit from owning their own homes in terms of forced savings (that part of their monthly mortgage that goes to paying off the principal).
3. They have some inflation protection.
4. They have security of tenure (they won't get kicked out by a Landlord).
5. They can customize their homes to their own individual tastes and needs.
6. They care more about their neighborhoods.
7. They are vigilant with respect to crime, vandalism and graffiti.
8. Home equity is the number one source of capital for starting a new business.
9. Home equity is also one of the most readily accessible emergency funds.

In North America, it has been the goal of government since the immediate post-war years to increase the percentage of the population who can own their own homes. This has been true in the US, Australia, New Zealand, Canada and many other nations. In fact, planning for post-war reconstruction began before the end of WWII—as early as 1943 and 1944 when it became apparent that Germany would likely lose the war.

Various government agencies have been in the business of guaranteeing or extending home mortgages for sub-prime borrowers for a long time—they usually do this through self-funding programs that add a point or so to the cost of home mortgages when you are a highly leveraged buyer (up to a 95% loan to value ratio).

In a scene from *It's a Wonderful Life*, lender George Bailey (played by the incomparable James Stewart) is arguing with archrival Mr Potter about whether working people should have access to high loan-to-value mortgages. It's worth watching that scene if for no other reason than to remember why our parents and grandparents organized institutions like savings and loans, co-ops, local banks, building societies, building and loan institutions, private lenders and sub prime insurers…

Ask most people how much money they can save and, if they are honest, they will tell you, "Not much." Even relatively good savers, once they have saved $5,000 or $10,000, can't resist spending it on a new PC, laptop, tablet, smartphone, vacation, new car, flat screen TV, what have you.

But most people will think twice about accessing their home equity for anything other than a major crisis or to start a new enterprise.

These days with unemployment still uncomfortably high, the thought of owning your own home and owning your own business, looks pretty good. I don't know about you, but I wouldn't like anyone tapping me on the shoulder and telling me, "We don't need or want you anymore, you're too old, and you're finished here…"

Of course, outplacement firms handle it better than this but don't tell me that what you hear and what they say are the same. What they say is, "Due to the overall economic situation that the company faces, you will have to find a job elsewhere. We have services such as CV preparation and an outplacement office you can visit every day and we have an industry-leading severance package for your review and, if you like, the review of your counsel."

What you actually hear is what I wrote above. It hurts, a lot. Politicians often say that they are immune to criticism. Don't believe a word of it. They are incredibly sensitive to negative stories about themselves. Employees are too.

More Analysis

Now it isn't hard to figure out what the Internal Rate of Return, IRR is for a sub-prime borrower in normal market conditions.

Let's say that your brother-in-law buys a $245,000 home with 5% down ($12,250), pays 4.5% for his mortgage and another 1% for insurance because he is a sub-prime borrower. He holds onto the house for five years and then sells. Real estate inflation is 2.25% p.a. and he "pays himself a rent" (this is called an imputed rent) of $1,675 per month.

You can look at the imputed rent as what he would have had to pay for a rental accommodation of similar quality for himself and his family.

Now under these assumptions, he bought the home for $245,000, he will sell it for $273,800 and he will pay some transaction fees (basically legal costs and real estate fees) of $14,492 so he nets around $259,339.

Remember he started with $12,250 and he ended up with $66,085 after five years, made up of: a) getting back his original equity of $12,250 when he sells the home, b) pay down of the mortgage principal of $37,254 (I used a 20 year amortization even though a 35 year amortization is often used in the US to lower monthly payments but significantly increases the total amount of interest over the mortgage lifecycle and significantly decreases the amount of principal paid down in the first years of the mortgage) and c) $28,831 from the increase in the value of his home less his original equity (don't double count).

Now you tell me, how many of your friends can save $66,692 in five years (or $63,843 if we ignore the contribution by imputed rent in years 1 to 5) and how many can make an IRR on their equity of 42.1% p.a.?

How about what happened to me—I gave a major private bank $100,000 in 1995 to invest for me in the bank's mutual funds. In the greatest stock market boom in the last 150 years (since the first days of the railroad revolution when everyone thought that there would be a railroad going to everyone's home and business and everyone bought speculative stock issues like they were buying a regular coffee for a nickel), the private bank *lost* $8,000 of my money. I never once got the promised monthly statement and when I finally insisted on a report in 2000, I realized they had churned my account over and over again and that they had four of the worst ten performing funds (out of 1,000 mutual funds). I asked for my money back—I told them I wasn't angry; just give me my money back. A monkey throwing darts at a chart of 1,000 mutual funds would certainly have done better. My father-in-law, Ken MacMillan, an old timer with a conservative bent, got the last laugh—he believed in cash.

I have uploaded my simple IRR model to my server and you can download it in .xls format from http://www.old.dramatispersonae.org/IRR/SampleIRR2-commercial.xls. I included a case where you have a more normal down payment of 25%.

In that second case, you put down $61,250 as your downpayment on the $245,000 home, your interest rate is lower (since you don't have to pay insurance for a high ratio mortgage), your imputed rent remains the same.

Now your IRR on your equity is lower (a still respectable 19.9%) and the cash in your jeans at the end of five years is $137,503 (or $107,633 if you ignore imputed rent).

You can see that, relatively speaking the high leverage home buyer has done better—your brother-in-law turned his $12,250 investment into $63,843 for a multiple of 5.2 while the more traditional homebuyer who put down $61,250 turned that into $107,633 for a multiple of 1.8. Both are good results but the higher leverage returned relatively more.

This points out an important fact—almost no one becomes wealthy from saving—the only way to wealth is via investing.

I also include in the spreadsheet a leverage summary—if you take your 25% down and buy five (rental) properties instead of one, you end up generating a ton more cash in five years: $197,307. Refer to the spreadsheet for details on how I calculate that.

Downside

Now for the downside: if the market goes down by more than 5%, you are upside down on equity. That means your equity is wiped out and lenders get very nervous. They may well refuse to renew your mortgage when your renewal comes up or will insist that you top up your equity so that, if they have to foreclose on the property or power of sale it, your equity may be wiped out but their loan is protected.

But in an uncertain market, you might find that the rental market actually ticks upward. As more lenders foreclose, more and more people will be in the rental market—afterall, they have to live somewhere. Rental vacancies might go down and rental rates might actually increase.

Upside

But I like to remember what Warren Buffett has said many times over the years—if you haven't sold in a down market, you haven't lost anything. So why worry?

This is also true in a down market in real estate. As long as your home or your rental portfolio can cashflow itself, stay with it. Real estate corrections happen but the overall market direction is up in North America usually by 2% p.a. or more over long periods of time.

There have been many downturns in the real estate market but it is still the one, time-tested way of creating wealth for yourself and your family.

Types of Return

As we have already seen, there are essentially three types of return in real estate:

a. cash on cash;
b. real estate inflation;
c. forced savings (this is a wealth effect) through the pay down of principal each month.

Cash on cash means that you are making some money from the property each month. You should never buy property that is cashflow negative on a monthly basis hoping that inflation or forced savings will bail you out.

Real estate inflation and the wealth effect both accrue to the equity holder. This is why comedian and actor Chris Rock has said, "King James is *rich* but the man who signs LeBron's paycheck is *wealthy*." If you control assets, you are wealthy or, at least, have the possibility of wealth.

Conclusion

I don't believe that sub-prime mortgagees are to blame for the financial meltdown in the marketplaces of the global economy. They are being unfairly blamed.

The folks on Wall Street who engineered complex financial products that practically nobody understood have a lot to account for. They sold sub-prime mortgages as mortgage-backed securities (MBS) or collateralized debt obligations (CDO) rated as if they were triple-A products. They made huge fees from selling them. Some of those same investment banks sold their own products short so when their value cratered, they made even more money. The people who bought them were stuck with millions of mortgages, some of which they couldn't even find the paper on. Try managing around that.

It is always the poorest members in our society who pay for the ridiculous bonuses and fees paid to these people. Sub-prime borrowers, who can least afford it, pay the highest interest rates on their mortgages, their credit cards, on OAC financing in stores, for services they buy—everyone builds in an extra risk margin for them.

Plus it is almost certainly the middle class, the poor and the SMEE sector who, through higher taxes and more costly services, have paid to bail out Wall Street investment bankers, hedge funds, insurance companies and major corporations who hire the best lobbyists and have enough political clout to protect themselves. It has happened before—when banks went out of their minds and loaned excessive amounts of money to Third World Nations in the 1980s (which were never paid back), ordinary people and SMEES paid about two points more to banks for the next ten years to restore the banks' capital bases.

We should not allow banks to foreclose on properties where borrowers have solid payment histories just because people on Wall Street have gotten frightened and decided to shut down their funds and call their loans. This is counter productive, smacks of panic, craters the resale and new home markets and undermines 60+ years of efforts to turn our countries into nations of homeowners.

@ProfBruce

[Prof Bruce is available for real estate coaching sessions. For more information, please contact Ms Nina Brooks, **ninabrooks@rogers.com**.]

ADDENDUM 1
Stocks or Real Estate, That is the Question?

By Brian Dagenais, founder, Brian Dagenais Properties

I often get asked how I got into the real estate business. Kicking, screaming and against my will would be the honest answer. Although I've been doing this since 2000, prior to that year, my attention was 100% focused on the stock market. I was quite happy to continue renting my tiny little 1-bedroom apartment, working full time at a rather ordinary job and flipping the channel between ROB and CNBC at every opportunity. It was an exciting time. Even though I earned significantly less than $30,000 per year, I was able to invest consistently and watch contributions of a few thousands of dollars turn into several tens of thousands of dollars in fantastically short periods of time. The mid to late 90s were great for investing in technology. I thought I was so smart and had my stock portfolio planned out to the year 2005, at which time I'd have in excess of a million dollars and would sell my portfolio, buy an interest bearing investment and live off the interest for the rest of my life—retired at age 34! Then my wife came along and ruined the party.

If we were to get married, we'd have to own a house, no more renting. I protested, "I don't have any money to buy a house. Check my bank account, there's $16 in it! No bank will qualify me for anything more than a tool shed." And then to my indignity, she pointed to my stock portfolio. There's lots of money there she insisted. Sell some of your stock. We almost didn't get married over it. I was devastated. I never had the discipline or the work ethic to do all that well in school and obtained only a very ordinary diploma from college. My stock portfolio represented my only opportunity to be wealthy in this life and here is this person telling me to start cashing it in early! Anyway, she won the argument.

A Brian Dagenais Property (circa 2013)

Thank goodness for that because I was able to actually buy two homes from the proceeds *before* the stock market crashed and eventually eroded what was left of my portfolio down to only a few thousand dollars. It was such a bizarre concept—a single share that was once worth well in excess of a hundred dollars, now only worth a couple of dollars a few years later. I was lucky enough to have sold most of my stock before it eroded away to nearly nothing but it was still a very sobering moment.

When I gave into my (now) wife, I assumed she'd want to buy a small single family home but she's an observant person and told me about some family friends that had bought rental properties in her home town and done very well over the span of a couple of decades. This husband and wife team had three children and when they got married, as a wedding gift, the parents bought each of them a small home in cash. That got my attention. After all, who pays cash for a house let alone three?

We ended up buying a small triplex, living in one unit and renting out the other two. I knew nothing about owning a home, even less about how to be a landlord. I was petrified. What if a toilet breaks at 2 am? What if tenants don't pay? What if they trash an apartment? I was ill equipped to handle such things. Luckily none of those things happened for the better part of a year. I seem to remember our first crisis being a leaky kitchen sink around 8 or 9 months into our ownership and miracle of miracles, I was able to fix it myself without calling a plumber. When I look back, that first 8 or 9 months of smooth sailing was so crucial to allowing me to continue and build upon this little venture of ours. Whatever else, your first investment *has* to work.

I think that if we had experienced road bumps early on, not being fully committed; I think I would have asked my wife to give up. But that didn't happen. And what did happen, which was very exciting— my mortgage balance shrunk rather quickly and noticeably. With a mortgage of $102,000 paying biweekly, I was able to cover the mortgage with my employment income, while my wife's income covered the rest of our bills. That left two rent cheques free to pay down the mortgage. And we did, and we bought another triplex six (!) months after buying our first using the remainder of my stock portfolio.

Over the next three years, we were able to pay down nearly 40% of the mortgage and appraisals of the property hinted at a little over $100,000 in price appreciation. I sat down and did the math— $100,000 in price appreciation and about $40,000 in mortgage pay down equaled about $140,000 in net worth built up over 36 months. And that was from just one property. What took me about five years to achieve in the stock market, I was able to achieve in about three from one property. After that appraisal, I was hooked; I was determined to push this as far as I could. Over the next several years, I bought a small single family home to flip in 2003, another triplex in 2005 and 2008, a fourplex in 2009 and a seven unit building in 2010. In 2012, I put an addition onto my smallest triplex, doubled the size and added a 4th unit to the building. It's been good by any standard but I'm always thinking it should be better.

Without a doubt, these investments have allowed me to live a lifestyle much better than if I had only employment income to draw on. That being said, I'm not rich, it hasn't been easy, it hasn't been quick, it's been frustrating at times and despite what the seminars and others may tell you, it's not idiot proof, it's not as passive as you think and although the income may grow in ways that please you, the expenses often grow more quickly than you ever expected. To this day, 13 years into this adventure, it is the "one-off" expenses; the unplanned expenses that never seem to stop and erode into your paper profit far more than you ever expected.

I invest for cashflow; properties that can support themselves without regular injections of cash out of my pocket. I do this because I look at a house and see it as a big hungry bear. It consumes a lot of resources. When things are going well and running properly, it's great to have the bear on your side. When things are bumpy and crashing down around you, that bear can be one giant burden. If the bear is self-sufficient, I feel far more comfortable in owning it as opposed to a bear that continuously digs into my pocket, wearing me down financially over time.

Maybe I expose myself too much to those Rich Dad, Poor Dad seminars that suggest you can be a millionaire in a few short years and a few short hours of work if you follow their advice or those TV renovation shows and get a little envious or frustrated when I see some office worker who's never used a hammer buy a run-down house and flip it for a $75,000 profit three months later. Unlike on TV, whenever I do a renovation, my bank, in all cases but one, values the property higher than prior to the renovation but only at a *fraction* of the money spent. My most recent renovation—a rather large project costing several hundreds of thousands of dollars only returned 60 cents on the dollar according to the bank's appraiser. I was hoping for 80 cents. We'll never know who is right until the property is sold but regardless, it was disappointing to see such good and seemingly thoughtful work only receive modest credit. By the way, I think the bank's appraiser is working for the bank not me so naturally, I believe he's wrong, I'm right.

I've been told that real estate is a passive form of investing and while I actually spend far more time at my 9-5 job, my real estate does occupy significant portions of my time, either requiring my presence or more often, simply requiring me to devote portions of my days and evenings planning, thinking, brainstorming on how to grow a more efficient business. While it is true that there are landlords out there that put little thought and attention into their properties and care little about their tenants, I like to go to bed with a clear conscience and truly believe that if you invest with an attitude towards quality and good customer service, it will pay off more often than not.

I've been a very fortunate landlord over the years. Starting with three units and working my way up to 24, I've had less than $6,000 in non-payment of rent. I've had but a tiny handful of midnight phone calls from tenants. I've had many tenants leave behind a big mess but I can only remember 1 or 2 incidents where I'd say they trashed the apartment. I did have one careless tenant cause a flood that did $17,000 in damage. At the time, I was very upset, feeling very worried and sorry for myself but looking back, I think I was able to actually turn it into a positive. Insurance covered the repair and returned to me an apartment that was actually better than the old one. They also covered the lost rent while the repair was taking place. I evicted the tenant and rented the repaired unit for 12% more than before. I guess that's a win but it certainly didn't feel that way at the time.

On the subject of evictions, I've had to do some but not as many as you might think—perhaps a half-dozen in 13 years and of those, only one fought me long and hard on it. One thing I've learned about this business is that you approve your tenants *slowly* but act *quickly* to remove them when appropriate. It's not a matter of being a nice guy, it's a matter of standards and I expect my tenants to rise to my standards as opposed to me bending to meet theirs. And in the vast majority of situations, it's worked.

Tenants can make you or break you in this business. People often ask me what I look for in choosing a tenant. I tell them I look to rent to people that have something to lose in life and by that I usually mean a verifiable job or in the cases of a young adult, an established parent. People with stable parents and stable jobs can be sued successfully. While there are no guarantees in this business, I find people with consistent and stable employment—verifiable employment—far less likely to take off in the middle of the night, far less likely to trash a unit or cause problems for others than compared to tenants with no job or *sporadic* employment. Someone with consistent and predictable employment likely has a fairly set routine in their lives. They are unlikely to want to disrupt it in any significant way by being a bad tenant and risking eviction. No guarantees though. The other thing I like to do is talk. I talk to my applicants. I try to get them to open up. We can talk about anything; it doesn't have to be solely about the apartment. In fact, aside from my sales pitch on the unit, I'd rather talk about just about anything else in their life. I find that the more I can get the applicant to talk, the better. I get a better understanding as to who they are as people; it gives me an idea as to how they'd fit in the apartment and with me and I also find that with potential tenants that have something to hide, in many cases, the more they talk, the more clues they give about their past. And since they may have something to hide, they're often exceedingly nice and likeable and when I find myself resolving gaps in their stories in my head because they're so nice, that's my warning sign that maybe I should pass on this person. It's not a perfect system and it takes time and practice but it works far more often than not in my experience.

As I've gained more experience, I've had more and more people come to me, most like to hear the story and a few want to get into it themselves. I'm always nervous giving advice because what works for me may not necessarily work for others. I was presented with a specific situation and opportunity and was able to plan, adjust and mold my actions slowly over many years. Each investor is going to have his or her own unique set of circumstances that will have to be taken into account. As such, I usually limit my advice to the advice I find that I give myself more and more recently—be patient, understand that you own the investment much more intimately than a stock and treat it as such; do not to be afraid to lose yourself providing customer service for your tenants. Dare to dream but be careful not to lie to yourself too often and accept disappointments and realities as they come and learn from them. I truly believe if you can follow these steps, you're very likely to be a satisfied investor over time.

Brian Dagenais, http://www.briandagenaisproperties.com/

Notes:
--Many small and medium sized Landlords use services to do background checks on prospective tenants. They can do: 1. employment verification, 2. credit check and 3. criminal record check. Costs usually range from

around $40 to $100. This can be well worth it. You can find them by searching for "background checks for landlords".

--One other thing that is highly recommended is regular, periodic checks of your units (giving tenants proper advance notice). These could be monthly but should not be less than quarterly. It helps further develop relationships with your tenants, gives advance warning of any problems with the units that need to be fixed and also provides an early warning that a tenant is turning into a problem.

ADDENDUM 2
Due Diligence

The process one goes through in purchasing a piece of real estate is remarkably similar to the process one utilizes to determine a site's highest and best use (http://www.eqjournal.org/?p=2155). It also resembles the process banks and other funders use to determine their risks from lending to a proposed (or existing) project.

Being Duly Diligent

What are some of the key things one has to do or look at when buying real estate, financing real estate or determining a site's highest and best use?

It's a valuable exercise for sellers of real estate as well as appraisers to undertake too. It can help them set a market price for their property as well as prepare for some objections that buyers might raise.

I can't believe how many sellers of real property do almost nothing to boost their case—many don't bother to prepare a comprehensive sales and marketing package. You would think that real estate agents would be very good at it but many are horribly unprepared to sell property.

I have bought (and sold) hundreds of properties and I have had the rather frustrating experience of asking a REALTOR or a seller basic questions like: what is the zoning on the property; what's the FSI (floor space index); what are the current rents and so forth and gotten... nothing.

Land and Buildings

When you buy real property that has existing buildings on it, you have just added more complexity. I tell my clients that the land under existing buildings is often more valuable if they remove the structures so, if they want to get full value for their properties, it is often best to pull down tired structures that are at the end of their economic lives and create a vacant lot.

Why is this? Well, sometimes it is because people can't visualize their own projects on a piece of land if there are other people's buildings 'in the way'. Humans are very territorial. That's why residential real estate agents who sell a lot of homes tell their clients not to leave anything personal around so that prospective buyers can visualize themselves and their stuff in the home not the current occupants. Same thing in commercial real estate, I am afraid.

Also, when you build something on a piece of land, you have locked in all the options for the foreseeable future (a life of 30 to 60 years is typical for commercial projects these days). It's just like when you buy a new car—you decide on the colour of the vehicle, engine size, whether it has a tow package, interior finishes, automatic or manual, etc. The moment you drive it off the lot, it devalues 15 to 30% overnight. If you drive it back to the dealer the next day because, say, you just lost your job, you will discover this for yourself.

There are the 'restocking charges' and the transaction costs to take into account but the biggest devaluation has taken place because you have locked in all the options, The person who next buys this vehicle might not like fire engine red or lemon yellow but they'll take it for a reduced price...

Same thing in buildings—there are thousands of small changes in the economy every year—so that a building built to meet one functional program (say, a roller disco rink) might not be suitable for a technology user a couple of years later when the disco craze dies. (I actually had this experience and the costs of retrofitting the building for a tech company after the roller disco place went bust were substantial.)

Most developers only think about form following function—they determine what the highest and best use is at one moment in time and then get an architect to wrap a form (i.e., a building) around those functions. But architects being the independent and stubborn people they are often disregard the developer anyway and design something that suits the site and the neighborhood—it grows organically from the ground, in a way. So function follows form; that means that they intuitively understand that a building will probably see a multitude of uses in its life.

Think it can't happen in residential construction? Think again. Imagine the computer cabling that a home like ours requires. Built if 1988, it had zero cabling for PCs. We now have five in our home and fishing the wire through walls and floors is hard and expensive.

Think about how many people work from home today or have home based business? It's phenomenal.

Think about how many baby boomers are going to need elder care soon, first for their parents, and then for themselves. I think that we are building homes that are wrong for the times—the whole industry needs a rethink but that is not the subject matter here.

Here are some due diligence questions for structures:

Have you had the building inspected?
Do you plan to tear down the existing building?
Can you get a demolition permit?
Are you going to renovate, rehabilitate or add to an existing structure?
How is the wiring, plumbing, roof, foundation, structure, etc.?
Are there any leases in place?
Are they long term or short term?
What are the rents?
Are they net, net, net leases (i.e., does the tenant pay all operating costs, property taxes and utilities)?
What operating costs will you have to pay?
Are the rents at, below or above market rents?
Which way is the rental market heading?
Who pays for major repairs such as structural repairs?
Who pays the property taxes?
Are there any inclusions or exclusions with the property (appliances, other chattels, fixtures, etc.)?
Are there any environmental or bio hazards (e.g., asbestos insulation, 'Legionnaires' disease)?
How are the HVAC (Heating, Ventilation and Air Conditioning) systems?
Are your operating costs above, at or below the norm for this type of real property?
Can you reduce your operating costs—are there any environmentally sustainable practices that you can implement?
Are the tenants sound financially?

Buying existing buildings is a lot like buying existing businesses. It takes a great deal more due diligence and a different mind set than building from scratch. Some people are really good at buying existing property or existing businesses and turning them around.

Those folks are often really bad at creating a new project so I would say that the industry is split between operators and constructors. I have been much more involved in the latter and I know that the skill set to build from nothing is quite different from the skill set to be a good operator.

Both can add a lot of value—the constructor can see a project in his or her mind's eye long before the first rivet is driven into the steel structure. They have a natural feel for the local market and what will work and they see things before other's do—they pioneer things.

A good operator can be creative too—they can see how it might be possible to add some 'lipstick' here and some 'makeup' there and create a whole new ambience. They can differentiate their projects on style, panache, quality, maintenance, clever redesign and use of space, etc. It isn't just that they mop the floors better than their competition.

Vacant Land

Real Estate is an industry where local knowledge is of paramount importance. Something that works well in Toronto and New York (say for the Reichman family of Olympia and York fame) may not work at all well in, say, London (at Canary Wharf, for example). Here are some of the things you should do or look at when buying vacant land:

What is the current zoning?
What is the current Official (or Master) Plan designation?
What types of uses are the adjacent lands being put to or contemplated?
How is the local economy doing?
What direction is the neighborhood heading in (is it stable, improving or deteriorating)?
What is the crime rate like in the vicinity including petty crime such as vandalism and graffiti?
How can you add value to this piece of real estate—what type of uses are most in demand?
What is the competition like?
Are other developers doing projects in the area?
How are they doing with those projects?
Is it possible that competition in the area could actually boost your proposed uses much as fast food restaurants or petrol stations flock together and feed off of each other (so to speak).
What kind of support (or opposition) are the neighbors likely going to give you for your proposed uses?
Have you talked to any of your neighbors?
What does your local councilor think of your project?
Have you walked the site, photographed it, developed a gut feeling for it?
Are your head, heart and gut all in agreement with your plan and offer to purchase?
Is the local infrastructure sufficient to support your project (storm water outlet, sewer capacity, piped water supply, road capacity, power,…)?
Are high speed Internet, cable and telephone service available?
Is public transit readily accessible?
Have you completed an economic feasibility study and rate of return calculation?
Does it meet your rate of return requirements?
How long will it take to get the project off the ground and realize this return?
Can you sustain the project if there are any delays?
Have you tested the economic feasibility of your project should there be any delays, cost overruns or changes in demand?
How can you tweak the project to either increase the benefits or decrease costs?
Have you spoken with city staff to gauge their level of support for your proposed uses?
Are there any wetlands on the property?
Is there any environmental contamination?
Are there any easements?
Does the Seller have clear title?
Is there any litigation affecting the property?
Can you get title insurance (http://www.old.dramatispersonae.org/TitleInsuranceExplained.html)?
Is this a freehold acquisition, long term land lease or a condo?
Can you obtain financing?
Will the Seller provide any financing (i.e., a STB, Seller Take Back mortgage)?
Can you get reasonably priced insurance?
Are there any heritage or archaeological constraints?
Have you met with officials from Provincial or State Ministries (environment, natural resources, transportation, agriculture, municipal affairs …)?
Are there any important natural resources on the property?
Are you purchasing riparian, subterranean and air rights too?
What are the setbacks and height limits affecting the property?

What are the building permit, development charge and other City, Province or State fees?
Have you had the property appraised by a professional appraiser?
Is the appraised value close to your proposed purchase price?
What are the property taxes?
What is the property's assessed value?
Are there any Tenancies and, if so, what is the income statement like and what is the capitalization rate and IRR?
Is there any deferred maintenance?
Is it a condo and, if so, what are the condo fees and is the condo corp solvent?
Are there any noise sources close by such as rail, car washes, turbines or high intensity industrial uses?
Are there any dangerous or noxious uses in close proximity (such as abattoirs, fire works factories, pulp and paper mills, petro chemical plants…)?
Are there any streams, water courses, navigable water ways that impact of the proposed uses for the site?
Is there enough room for parking and park land?
Are there any short term or long term land leases (such as agricultural uses or parking uses) that impact the lands?
Can you get vacant possession of the lands?
Are there any residential tenancies and, if so, can you get evictions if you need vacant possession?
Can you get vehicular access to the property, road cut permits or culvert permits?
Can you take down trees if you need to?
Can you get full left in, left out access for vehicles?
If the property is being developed on private services, is there potable water on the site?
Can you install a septic system on the site?
Why is the Seller selling?
Can you obtain a survey?
Does the survey show all easements, encroachments and rights-of-way?
Is the APS (Agreement of Purchase and Sale) subject to any excise fees (land transfer taxes, Goods and Services Taxes, HST, VAT (Value Added Taxes), withholding taxes for non-residents…)?
Are the property taxes up to date?
Is the property subject to foreclosure, power of sale conditions and rights of redemption?
Are there any liens on the property or other encumbrances?
Is the property subject to any rights of first refusal?
What did the Seller originally pay for the lands and when?
What did neighboring lands sell for?

I am sure there are many more due diligence questions that we could come up with but this is a good start.

Buying real property is hard. Many, many people make mistakes in this business so getting it right the first time is pretty important.

About the Author

Bruce M Firestone
B Eng (Civil), M Eng-Sci, PhD

Bruce applied to go to McGill University in Montreal at age 14, arrived after turning 15, and graduated as a civil engineer before legally becoming an adult (then, age 21). He was rejected in his first job search because he was considered a "child," not legally responsible for his actions. Three and a half weeks later, he was living in Sydney, Australia. A new and exciting labour government had just been elected. The first two things Prime Minister Gough Whitlam did were to recall Aussie troops from Vietnam and to lower the age of majority to 18.

Bruce worked for the New South Wales government, doing operations research and building mixed integer programming models while continuing his education at the University of New South Wales, where he obtained his Masters of Engineering-Science degree, and then at the Australian National University in Canberra, where he received his PhD in urban economics.

He was among the first group in Australia to fly hang-gliders and not die. He has traveled to and worked in the United States, Sri Lanka, New Zealand, India, Canada, Australia and many other nations. He has been, at different times, an engineer, a real estate developer, a hockey executive (founder of NHL team the Ottawa Senators, Canadian Tire Centre and the Senators Foundation—a children's charity), a university professor, a keynote speaker, a consultant, coach, mentor, art collector and benefactor, writer, columnist, futurist, and novelist as well as Executive Director of not-for-profit Exploriem.org—an organization dedicated to assisting entrepreneurs, artpreneurs, and intrapreneurs everywhere. Bruce went back to school in his 50s, completed eight real estate courses and is now a real estate broker with Century 21 Explorer Realty Inc.

Bruce has taught and studied at McGill University, Laval University, the University of New South Wales, the Australian National University, Harvard University, the University of Western Ontario, Carleton University, and the University of Ottawa in subject areas that include entrepreneurship, business models, architecture, engineering, finance, urban planning, urban design, traffic and transportation planning, and development economics.

He has launched, or helped launch, more than 300 startups. Currently, he writes for three blogs—EQJournal.org (about entrepreneurship), DramatisPersonae.org (about artpreneurship and urban issues) and profbruce.tumblr.com (about life)—and moderates lively @ProfBruce and @Quantum_Entity communities on Twitter. He is also author of *Quantum Entity Trilogy*, *Real Estate Investing Made Easy*, *How to get Rich for Real*, *How to Retire Rich at Any Age, For Real*, and *Entrepreneurs Handbook II*. His upcoming novels include *Urban Nirvana and the Peradventures of Maddy Henderson*, and *Saragasso City*.

He is married to a most wonderful girl, Dawn MacMillan. They have five great kids and one fine grandson.

...

"Entrepreneurs follow a moral path when they—first, take care of their business so that, second, the business can take care of their families so that, third, their families can take care of them so that, fourth, they don't become a burden on society or their fellow human beings so that, fifth, they can help others so that, sixth, others can help their business," Prof Bruce, 2014.

His current motto is: "*Making the impossible, possible*".

...

Blogs: eqjournal.org, dramatispersonae.org and www.profbruce.tumblr.com
Twitter: @ProfBruce and @Quantum_Entity
LinkedIn: www.linkedin.com/in/profbruce
Facebook: https://www.facebook.com/QuantumEntityTrilogy
YouTube: http://www.youtube.com/user/ProfBruce and http://www.youtube.com/user/quantumentitytrilogy
Books available from: http://www.brucemfirestone.com

...

How to Retire Rich at Any Age, For Real

Developed nations are divided into three classes—people, mostly government workers, with defined benefit pension plans, the top 1% who in 2012 had a 19.3% share of US national income (up from just 7.7% in 1973) and everyone else.

This book is written for the latter—the 80% of the working population who have to fend for themselves.

Bruce M Firestone looks at the case of Ms Maya Yates, a 36 year old single mother with a decent job who has set a goal of retiring by age 62 with an income similar to what she is currently earning. When she discovers that she will need to save $6.7 million over the next 26 years to reach her goal (equivalent to putting away more than 3 times her current annual salary every year), Maya comes to Firestone looking for alternatives; together they come up with a plan to enable her to acquire a mini real estate empire so she can realistically provide for herself and her three children.

@profbruce

www.ingramcontent.com/pod-product-compliance
Lightning Source LLC
Chambersburg PA
CBHW040845180526
45159CB00001B/320